REIMAGINING YOUR NONFICTION PICTURE BOOK

A STEP-BY-STEP REVISION GUIDE

KIRSTEN W. LARSON

BOTHARD BOOKS

ENDORSEMENTS

"*Reimagining Your Nonfiction Picture Book* is a must-have for every nonfiction picture book writer's bookshelf. Chapter after chapter helps demystify the process of writing and revising a nonfiction picture book [to] help it stand out in agents' or editors' inboxes. Larson's conversational tone is easy to understand yet in depth enough to help every writer. With examples from her own process of writing and revising her published picture books, writers can work through the entire revision process with one of their own manuscripts. Her exercises at the end of each chapter provide easy-to-follow guidelines for every nonfiction picture book they write. I highly recommend this book!"

—Debra Shumaker, author of *Freaky, Funky Fish, Peculiar Primates,* and *Tell Someone*

"Fact-loving kidlit writers will love *Reimagining Your Nonfiction Picture Book.* Kirsten W. Larson delivers detailed information, examples, and hands-on exercises in these inspiring pages. Larson comes alongside writers who are ready to take their nonfiction manuscript to new levels as they explore structures and scenes, voice and tension, text features and so much more. She packed the wisdom, inspiration, and experience of a writing conference into these pages. Highly recommend!"

—Annette Whipple, author of *The Truth About* series

BOOKS BY KIRSTEN W. LARSON

NONFICTION PICTURE BOOKS

Wood, Wire, Wings: Emma Lilian Todd Invents an Airplane (Calkins Creek Books)

A True Wonder: The Comic Book Hero Who Changed Everything (Clarion Books)

The Fire of Stars: The Life and Brilliance of the Woman Who Discovered What Stars Are Made Of (Chronicle Books)

COMING SOON

This Is How You Know (Little, Brown Books for Young Readers)

The Light of Resistance (Roaring Brook Press)

OTHER NONFICTION BOOKS FOR YOUNG READERS

The Sloth: Living with Less (Heinemann Publishing Company)

Robotics in Our World series, four books (Amicus Publishing)

The Second Amendment: The Right to Bear Arms (Capstone Press)

International Space Station (Rourke Educational Media)

Protecting Our People series, six books (Amicus Publishing)

The Rock Cycle (Rourke Educational Media)

Tools of the Trade: Using Scientific Equipment (Rourke Educational Media)

Statistics about U.S. Special Ops, Past and Present (Capstone Press)

Freaky Nature series, four books (Amicus Publishing)

The West: Arizona, California, Nevada (Mason Crest)

Tsunamis (Rourke Educational Media)

Nuclear Meltdowns (Rourke Educational Media)

Skunk Science (Schoolwide, Inc.)

The Balloon Brothers (Schoolwide, Inc.)

Mars's Rolling Robot (Schoolwide, Inc.)

The Hairy Spider (Schoolwide, Inc.)

To Catch a Comet (Schoolwide, Inc.)

Science Fair Success! (Rourke Educational Media)

Using the Scientific Method (Rourke Educational Media)

CONTENTS

INTRODUCTION

Are you struggling with a nonfiction picture book draft? Is there a gap between the book in your head and what you poured onto the page? Does your story feel flat or lack the emotion and excitement you know it could hold?

Maybe your critique group, an agent, or an editor has told you your book isn't quite "there" yet but didn't provide specifics. Or you're facing the opposite problem and are sifting through conflicting feedback. Or you're just getting started, and you have a true story you desperately want to tell, but no clue where to start. You've done a ton of research but haven't put pen to paper. Now what?

If any of these scenarios sound like you, you've come to the right place. While this book assumes you have already written a nonfiction picture book draft, you'll find a wealth of advice whether you're on your first draft or your fiftieth—or even if you haven't written a draft at all.

Today's **trade** nonfiction requires a high level of craftsmanship. This includes strong concepts, ample heart, and meaningful takeaways to maximize re-readability. It requires innovative structure, perfect pacing, captivating voice, and strong illustration potential. Today's nonfiction also demands strong **back matter** that adds to the book's usefulness in classrooms and libraries. All of these topics are covered here.

For the last few years, I've taught a workshop version of *Reimagining Your Nonfiction Picture Book* at The Writing Barn. Through working with my students and private coaching clients, I realized the need for a book that went deeper into the writing craft topics mentioned above.

This book is intended to fill the gap between classics like Ann Whitford Paul's *Writing Picture Books*, which covers craft but is fiction focused, and *Anatomy of Nonfiction* by Margery Facklam and Peggy Thomas, which is a broad survey of children's nonfiction from magazines to picture books, middle grade, and more.

My focus is trade nonfiction picture books, which are published by major publishers like Simon & Schuster; Little, Brown and Company; and Penguin Random House, as well as medium and smaller publishers like Scholastic, Chronicle Books, Millbrook Press, and Calkins Creek Books. These titles are meant to be read by an adult to children. You will find them for sale in bookstores as well as online.

This book *doesn't* cover **school and library nonfiction**, also called educational nonfiction. School and library nonfiction is frequently published in series and written at specific reading levels so children can read the books on their own. Often authors are hired to write these books according to specifications the publisher provides, in a process called work for hire. You don't normally find these books for sale at bookstores; they are sold directly to schools and libraries. To learn more about the educational market, see Laura Purdie Salas's *Writing for the Educational Market.*

Whether you're a seasoned nonfiction author or exploring nonfiction for the first time, welcome! I'm excited to have you here. As you work through this book, always remember that kids need your stories. Your nonfiction picture book has the power to affect young readers deeply, to reflect and expand their worlds, to capture their curiosity, and to inspire them.

I'll give you the revision toolbox. You bring the persistence. Together we'll get your passion onto the page.

WHO AM I?

I'm a writer who shares the same challenges you do. As I tell my writing students, it took me a long time to learn how to write nonfiction picture books. *Wood, Wire, Wings*, my first published picture book, only sold after a **revise-and-resubmit (R&R)** request from my editor, Carolyn Yoder. And even then, I had to revise multiple times after the project was **acquired**. Through that process, I learned how to write in scenes, put readers in the head of my main character, get emotion onto the page, and reinforce a book's takeaway. Writing *Wood, Wire, Wings* taught me so much about the power of revision.

WHO AM I? (THE RESUMÉ EDITION)

I've been writing nonfiction books for young readers for more than ten years. I've published three nonfiction picture books for the trade market, with additional picture books and a graphic novel under contract. My publishers include Astra Publishing House/Calkins Creek Books; HarperCollins/Clarion Books; Chronicle Books; Hachette Book Group/Little, Brown and Company; and Macmillan Publishers/Roaring Brook Press.

I've also written thirty nonfiction books for the school and library market for readers of all ages, as well as numerous magazine articles for kids.

I started life as a journalist in college, writing for two daily newspapers, plus my college daily. Though I loved journalism, I didn't love the late nights. So, when I graduated, I went to work for NASA in public relations. I wrote press releases and video scripts, ran press conferences, and trained NASA leaders to meet the media. I learned how to communicate complicated science and engineering ideas and breakthroughs in a way everyday people could understand. It was great training for conveying complicated **STEM** (science, technology, engineering, and math) concepts for kids through nonfiction picture books.

I'm also a passionate writing instructor and coach. As I mentioned earlier, I've worked with dozens of students through my "Reimagining

Your Nonfiction Picture Book" course at The Writing Barn and other webinars. I've also taught "Noodling with Nonfiction Picture Book Structure" for the 12x12 Picture Book Challenge.

I also personally coach writers of informational books using the same tools this book shares. My goal—always—is to help you bring your vision for your story to life. I appreciate your trust. And I congratulate you on taking the important step of reading this book.

Now let's get started.

———

How to Access the Resources Mentioned in This Book

Throughout *Reimagining Your Nonfiction Picture Book*, I mention many resources that may prove helpful during your revision process. I have put links to all of them on my website: https://KirstenWLarson. com/NFPBLinks/. If you find a broken link, please let me know through the contact form on my website so I can update it. Thank you!

SECTION 1: FIRST STEPS

CHAPTER 1

ARE YOU REALLY READY TO REVISE?

Revising is hard work. Revisiting the same story over and over takes stamina. To keep yourself motivated, you need a clear understanding of why your story matters to you—and, by extension, why it will matter to young readers.

After reading Chapter 1 you will:

- Remember your story spark
- Reignite your emotional connection to your story
- *Or* decide to let your story go

REVISING BUTTERFLIES

By May 2023, I was ready to give up. According to my agent, my current project needed yet another round of revision.

Normally I love the revision process! Sure, it might take me a few days or a few weeks, but typically I can envision a new way forward for my stories.

This time was different. I couldn't marshal any enthusiasm to try the story one more way. I had been working on this project off and on for five years. It had begun as a book about the butterfly effect. It had morphed into a book about biodiversity. One editor had liked my initial butterfly effect take but wanted an overall **narrative** instead of a series of vignettes. Another said I should switch from an informational story to a nonfiction book about real butterfly species.

There was a lot of conflicting feedback pointing my manuscript in different directions. And worst of all, I had lost touch with what I wanted the story to be. I had lost my story spark, something that always serves as my internal compass. I know that when I lose my spark, the resulting writing will be bad. *Very* bad. It was time to stop and remember why I'd started this story in the first place.

STORY SPARKS

When you first have a story idea, it often feels like a lightning strike. There's an energy, an enthusiasm. You write and research late into the night. Maybe you get up before everyone else in your house, delighting in the writing over cups of coffee.

You are convinced this is the best idea ever! *This* is the story that will get you an agent. *This* is the story that will finally sell or get starred reviews or win awards. No matter what else you are doing, you can't wait to sit down at the keyboard or your writer's notebook and get going.

But somewhere along the way, your spark starts to flicker. Maybe you hit research roadblocks. Or your pages read like an encyclopedia entry. Maybe people give you conflicting feedback. That's what happened to me. It's so easy to give up and move on to the next idea.

You can get your story back on track, but you will need to remember why you started it in the first place.

EXERCISE 1: JOURNALING YOUR STORY SPARK

Take out your writer's notebook and answer the following questions:

- What was your original story spark or inspiration for the story? How did the idea come to you?

- What did it feel like to land on this idea? What made you excited to write it in the first place? Take yourself back to that moment of discovery and write down everything you can remember about it.
- Why are you passionate or curious about this topic? Why do you think it resonates with you so strongly?
- What are some things you love about your story? This last question comes from Allison K. Williams in her revision book, *Seven Drafts*, which I highly recommend for novelists. Even when our stories are being super troublesome, there is always something to love in them. It's good to remind ourselves of that.

Now open your current draft and type two or three sentences summarizing your answers to the above questions at the top of the first page of your manuscript. That way, you will see it each and every time you open your document to revise.

There. Is the spark burning brighter now? Has some of the energy and enthusiasm returned? I hope so.

THE CHOICE TO MOVE ON—FOR NOW OR FOR GOOD

Writers set projects aside for all kinds of reasons. Sometimes a book is just not right for the current market. Maybe too many books have been published recently on your topic. In that case, you might set the book aside for a time.

This has happened to me. Years ago, I desperately wanted to publish a picture book biography of Jane Austen. I have boxes of research and stacks of books to prove my love for Jane Austen and her works (not to mention DVDs of the movie and miniseries versions of *Pride and Prejudice* and all the other books). But when three different authors came out with picture books about Austen in a short span of time, I couldn't see a way forward, at least for now.

Sometimes a story spark is gone for good. Elizabeth Gilbert talks about this in her inspirational book *Big Magic*, which is one of my all-time favorite writing books. Gilbert recounts losing her spark for her novel set in the Amazon jungle after she shelved it temporarily to focus on another book. She was never able to come back to it and abandoned the project for good. If best-selling author Elizabeth Gilbert of *Eat, Pray, Love* fame can lose her way, it can happen to any of us.

If you've decided to move on, for now or forever, congrats. You've learned something just by going through the process of researching, writing, and revising to this point. Hopefully your next project will be the one whose spark ignites you and carries you all the way through.

BACK TO THE BUTTERFLIES

You may be wondering what happened to my butterfly/biodiversity story.

I went through the exact same process I shared with you in Exercise 1. I remembered what I loved about the story and why I wanted to share it with young readers. And I realized it wasn't a biodiversity story.

I had a heartfelt conversation with my agent. We discussed returning to an earlier draft, which only one editor had seen and rejected. That was the story that captured my story spark.

My agent agreed to send it to editors.

Will the story sell? Who knows? All we can control is the work itself.

At least I feel like I told the story I wanted to tell, in the best way I could. Are you ready to do the same for your manuscript?

CHAPTER 2
FORGET "JUST THE FACTS"

A picture book has to stand up to multiple readings. What gives a story re-readability isn't just the facts it conveys. Kids can get those on the internet. To make a manuscript book-worthy, you have to offer a surprising take on the facts and let the reader know why they should care.

After reading Chapter 2, you will:

- Understand what a takeaway is
- Know the surprising take on the facts you are offering and why it should matter to a reader
- Be able to summarize your takeaway in a single sentence so you know what you are writing toward

THE KITCHEN SINK

I like to call my early drafts "kitchen sink" drafts. They are cluttered with names, dates, places, and all kinds of extraneous facts guaranteed to put my poor readers to sleep. They certainly don't do much to convince kids why they should care about the story. Instead, they read like school reports or encyclopedia entries.

Do you want to see what I mean? Here's a snippet from one of the earliest drafts of what became *Wood, Wire, Wings*, illustrated by Tracy Subisak:

Adventure called. Miss Todd moved to Pennsylvania, New York, and then St. Louis, where she worked for the 1904 World's Fair. The Wright brothers had flown for the first time in 1903, and St. Louis buzzed with flying mania. Captain Baldwin's big balloon, called a dirigible, rose into the sky. Gliders grazed the clouds. And Lilian Todd's apartment overlooked the airfield. Her view ignited a burning desire to conquer the air herself.

Back in New York, a friend showed Miss Todd a newspaper clipping from France. In 1906, a boxy biplane, called the "Bird of Prey," soared successfully. Miss Todd took one look and knew she could do better.

Look at all those names, dates, and places! Reading this passage now, I can see that the facts distract from the main story of a woman inspired by the latest in airplane designs to create something of her own.

Today, I can give myself a little grace when a paragraph like the above tumbles out. I know the kitchen sink draft is simply a starting point. I have to get all the facts out of my system before I can figure out two crucial things:

- The point I am making
- Why kids should care

Taken together, these are my takeaway. It's what I want to leave young readers with when they close the book. Finding your takeaway is the first step to reimagining your story.

Here are the takeaways from a few of my books:

- *Wood, Wire, Wings*: You have to fail to succeed—that's the engineering design process.

- *A True Wonder: The Comic Book Hero Who Changed Everything*, illustrated by Katy Wu: Heroes come in all shapes and sizes, and we can all be heroes of our own stories.
- *The Fire of Stars: The Life and Brilliance of the Woman Who Discovered What Stars Are Made Of*, illustrated by Katherine Roy: Curiosity and persistence are what make a great scientist.

WHY DO YOU NEED A TAKEAWAY?

Books are expensive. Just look at the list price on a few picture books from your shelf. They often cost close to twenty dollars. If a caregiver, teacher, or librarian is buying a book, they want it to be read multiple times, not read once and never picked up again.

To make a book worthy of multiple readings, it must present a new idea to your reader that goes beyond just the facts. It must speak to your readers' hearts and elicit strong emotions. It must create surprise and delight in your readers by presenting information in a fresh way. Remember, your book is competing with free facts available via any internet-connected computer, tablet, or phone.

EXERCISE 2: DETECTING TAKEAWAYS

I'm a big fan of using mentor texts to study all kinds of craft elements. Studying mentor texts is a fancy way of saying, "reading picture books like a writer." You can read picture books to learn about structure, voice, beginnings, endings, and so much more. You can study them to learn about takeaways, too.

When picking mentor texts, it's best to select books currently being produced, not classics that were popular ten, twenty, or even thirty years ago. Tastes change, and nonfiction picture books written today are very different from earlier books. Try to select books that have been produced in the last five years. To find when a book was published, look at the copyright date on the publishing information page.

To help you analyze mentor texts, I've provided a worksheet in

Appendix C. You'll also find the worksheet available for download on the resources page on my website.

When you read a picture book, make sure to read the dedications, author's note, and **jacket flap copy**, too. (The jacket flap copy is the marketing copy on the inside of the book jacket.) All these elements often hint at an author's takeaway. After you read the mentor text, answer the following questions:

- What's the author's point?
- Why should a child care about this story? And why would it matter to a child and their world?
- What's the one thing a child reader should take away from the story?
- What's the one message they should remember after they close the book?

Now summarize the author's point and why it matters in a sentence or two. That's the takeaway.

Here are the takeaways from a few of my favorite nonfiction books:

- *Survivor Tree* by Marcie Colleen, illustrated by Aaron Becker: We can all survive hard things (the power of resilience).
- *Pipsqueaks, Slowpokes, and Stinkers: Celebrating Animal Underdogs* by Melissa Stewart, illustrated by Stephanie Laberis: What some people see as a weakness is really a strength (the power of underdogs).
- *Animal Architects* by Amy Cherrix, illustrated by Chris Sasaki: Animals can shape their environments and homes just like human architects.

It's good practice to summarize the takeaway for each book you read. Through time, you'll notice many books have the same takeaway. Almost every picture book biography is in some way about the power of persistence. Lots of nonfiction books feature everyday heroes, or kids with the power to change the world, especially when they work together. You might even find it helpful to keep a list of common takeaways you find in nonfiction picture books. That way, when you are trying to find your takeaway, you can reference this list to help spark some ideas.

YOUR TAKEAWAY

Now take out your work in progress and your writer's notebook. Answer these three questions about your draft:

- What do you want readers to remember when they close your book? Go beyond just the facts.
- What do you want them to feel or do in response to your story?
- In the words of Lisa Cron in *Story Genius*, "What's your point?"

Now write your takeaway to summarize the point you are making and why kids should care.

If you get stuck, it might be helpful to look at your story spark from Exercise 1 to see how you connect emotionally to the story. Remember that you, the author, are a stand-in for your reader. What surprises and delights you or moves you to tears will likely do the same for your reader.

Here's one big caveat when it comes to nonfiction takeaways: your research must support whatever takeaway you choose. For example, the takeaway of *Wood, Wire, Wings* is, "You have to fail to succeed." That takeaway wouldn't have worked if Lilian Todd succeeded in building her airplane on the very first try. But I compiled evidence of her many struggles and failures, so my takeaway fits. Your takeaway must be backed up by your facts.

If you are still struggling with your takeaway, try this short exercise. First, picture your reader. Now imagine yourself telling this child why they should be excited to read your book and what they will learn from it. Then, write it down.

WHEN THERE'S NO TAKEAWAY

Of course, when it comes to takeaways, there are always exceptions. Nonfiction aimed at the school and library market often doesn't have a takeaway beyond "just the facts." Melissa Stewart and Marlene Correia call these books "traditional nonfiction" in their book, *5 Kinds of Nonfiction*. Active nonfiction like kids' craft books or cookbooks also don't have a takeaway. Neither do browsable nonfiction books from publishers like DK Books or National Geographic Books on vast topics like Egypt or Ancient Greece that are packed with pictures, text boxes, and other **text features**. To learn more about these types of nonfiction, check out the link to Melissa Stewart's website that I've included in the resources list on my website.

Still, if your goal is to submit your nonfiction book to a trade publisher, you must make a point or offer a unique take that will stick with readers long after they close the book. You must tap into emotion and surprise, not just curiosity.

Now that you know what point your book is making, let's see how it shapes your book's structure.

————

REMEMBERING YOUR READER

When analyzing picture books, including your own, it's important to ask, "How will the child see themselves reflected in this story, and how will they connect to it?" Often the takeaway is how a child connects to the story. Sometimes they will see themselves on the page in the visual story, even if no child is mentioned in the text. That's what happens in the book *Fry Bread: A Native American Family Story* by Kevin Noble Maillard, illustrated by Juana Martinez-Neal. The child might identify with the topic, perhaps a kid favorite like construction vehicles, or they might be inspired by the sense of wonder the story evokes. As you study mentor texts, always consider the child reader and note what makes the book child appropriate.

SECTION 2: STORY STRUCTURES

CHAPTER 3
MAKING YOUR POINT

Both kids' attention spans and picture books are short. Nonfiction picture books are thirty-two or forty pages and often 1,000 words or fewer. With that kind of space, you can't include every fact, figure, and vignette. Instead, you have to choose examples and events that support your takeaway from the very first page.

After reading Chapter 3, you will:

- Understand how your takeaway shapes what information you include in your draft
- See how your takeaway influences your book's starting point

PLOT PROBLEMS

Like many picture book biographers, I had a problem.

My subject, Emma Lilian Todd, the first woman to design a working airplane on her own, had done a lot of cool stuff. She had built an airplane, of course. But before that, she had also been one of the first women to work in the Pennsylvania government. She had been part of the first women's law class at New York University. And she had started the Junior Aero Club in America, an early maker space she ran out of her apartment to teach kids the science of flight. Surely, all these accolades needed to be in a biography about Emma Lilian Todd.

So that's what I did: I put them all in the book.

And then I realized my mistake.

Most of these events had little to do with my takeaway that you have to fail to succeed, and that failure is a perfectly normal part of the engineering process.

Did being in the women's law class fit with this idea? Nope.

How about working in the Pennsylvania government? Not at all.

Founding the Junior Aero Club? Sadly, no. (That fact got punted to the back matter, often a perfect home for extraneous fun facts.)

I was beginning to realize how my takeaway could help me wrangle my plot. Let's take a closer look.

THREE BEE BOOKS

Below are three books on a single topic. (You will find a full list of every book mentioned in this book in Appendix B.) Each has a unique takeaway that shaped what the authors included as examples in their books:

- *Give Bees a Chance* by Bethany Barton
- *Honeybee: The Busy Life of* Apis Mellifera by Candace Fleming, illustrated by Eric Rohmann
- *If Bees Disappeared* by Lily Williams

In *Give Bees a Chance*, Barton's takeaway is that bees are helpful and mostly not harmful to humans. In other words, we should give bees a chance. (The takeaway is right in the title!) Her examples include some facts that show how fascinating bees are, why they sting, how to protect ourselves from stings (so we won't be scared), and how useful bees are at pollinating. She ends with the idea that bees need our help.

Contrast that with Candace Fleming's *Honeybee*, which Fleming has called a biography of a bee. The takeaway for this book is that even seemingly small, unimportant creatures have busy, important lives. Because this is written like a biography, Fleming chooses events that show the full life of a bee from birth to death. In contrast, Barton doesn't include any information about how bees are born and die in her book.

Birth and death aren't mentioned in Lily Williams's book either. Williams's point is that small changes in our environment, like the potential disappearance of bees, can have huge consequences for our whole world. She begins by explaining that bees are a keystone species. Her examples include the jobs bees do, like pollination, and how they function in a hive. With that background, she explains what threatens bees and how the disappearance of bees would cascade through the ecosystem, affecting plant pollination, development of fruits, and the populations of birds that eat those fruits. The resulting trophic cascade would affect our entire world. She ends with a hopeful message of how we can help bees and prevent such a disaster.

EXERCISE 3: SAME TOPIC, MULTIPLE TELLINGS

Now it's your turn to grab two or three picture books about Ada Lovelace or sharks or any other topic from your local library and answer the following for each book:

- What's the author's point or takeaway?
- What events and examples does each book share?
- Which events and examples are different among the books?
- Which examples and events are the same?
- Why do you think the authors made those choices?

As you study these books, you can see how the authors' points interact with their respective choices about what facts to include. Now let's see how that might work for your book.

USING YOUR POINT TO SHAPE YOUR BOOK

Once you have your takeaway in place, it can serve as the literal endpoint for your book. Your whole book and everything you share with the reader will help them learn that takeaway by the time they close the cover.

For example, in a narrative like a biography or history story, the main character serves as the reader's stand-in, or avatar. In other words, the child reader lives the events of the book through the eyes of the main character. That main character has a big goal they want to achieve. The plot events are made up of the steps they take to achieve the goal, what happens as a result, and how the main character reacts. Those plot events cause the character to make choices, change, and learn the takeaway by the end of the book.

But this brings up some questions. What was the main character like in the beginning of the story? Where does their journey start before they learn their lesson? That starting point should be as far away as possible from where the main character winds up. That way, their journey can be long and difficult and filled with ups and downs—those plot events—that will help them learn the takeaway.

"Plot" is quite different in **expository** literature, which doesn't have a main character. Melissa Stewart defines expository literature as books on narrowly defined topics that "feature an innovative format and carefully chosen text structure, a strong voice, and rich, engaging language." In expository literature, readers are the ones who change and come to a new understanding by reading the book. The takeaway is still an endpoint and likely makes up the last **spread** of the picture book. So where is your reader at the beginning? What assumptions or misbeliefs are they toiling under? What examples will best make your point and change your reader's thinking about your topic?

In nonfiction, we don't make things up, but we do get to choose where to start the journey and where to end it. We choose what examples and plot events contribute to the point we are trying to make. If you don't know your point, you can't know your plot. The result will be a draft with a lot of extraneous fluff. Or, dare I say it, a kitchen sink. You don't want that!

Next let's look at some different ways you can arrange events and examples using different **story structures**. The Western, three-act narrative is just one of many options.

CHAPTER 4
NAILING THE NARRATIVE

People have a natural affinity for narratives, especially adults like teachers, librarians, and parents who do most of the book buying. Because narrative structure is so popular, it can be a good fit for many stories, not just traditional biographies about people (remember *Honeybee*?). Most narratives follow a predictable story structure that isn't hard to learn.

After reading Chapter 4, you will:

- Understand the key elements of narrative structure
- Know if narrative structure is a potential fit for your book
- Ensure you are hitting the major narrative beats

THE APPEAL OF NARRATIVE

My client Nicole's book was falling a bit flat (Note: Client's names have been changed to protect their privacy.). It didn't have the energy and emotion her agent thought it needed to sell. The agent devised a common solution: turn the expository book into a narrative book.

This is fairly common feedback writers get from critique partners, agents, and editors, who tend to gravitate to narratives. A narrative is a story that conveys an experience versus just the facts. It starts with "once upon a time" and ends with "the end."

Some scholars argue that the bias toward narratives is part of how humans evolved. In *On the Origin of Stories*, scholar Brian Boyd argues that narratives are like child's play for the mind. Like play, stories serve an evolutionary purpose: to show us how others experience the world, to create empathy, and ultimately to help children learn lessons that ensure their survival. Author Lisa Cron assures us humans are *Wired for Story*, as her book title says.

Research shows that grown-ups have a clear preference for narratives. Author Melissa Stewart has done some polling on the topic. Her data shows that 56 percent of gatekeepers like teachers and librarians prefer narrative books, while 36 percent like narrative and expository literature equally (Stewart and Correia in *5 Kinds of Nonfiction*). But for children, the data is quite different: 25 percent prefer narrative and 33 percent like narrative and expository literature equally. That means 42 percent have a clear preference for expository literature.

I'm not here to discuss the merits of narrative versus expository nonfiction, but the data is clear: adults, who often select books for children, prefer narratives. For a fuller exploration of the topic, see Melissa Stewart's articles for educators, which you'll find linked on my website.

So what does that mean for a writer? Once you have established your takeaway (your point) and chosen which events and examples to include from your research, you might try out narrative structure for your story. It's not the only choice, as you'll see in Chapters 5 and 6, but it is a popular one.

NARRATIVE IN A NUTSHELL

Here are the essential elements of a narrative, which we'll discuss one at a time:

- A main character
- A story goal, quest, or problem

- A change in the main character from beginning to end,
  known as the **character arc**

Main Character

The main character is the stand-in for the child reader in the book. When you read a story, it's like you're inhabiting the mind of the main character. You experience the plot events from their perspective.

Most of the time, the main character is a person. In fact, narrative is a popular structure for picture book biographies. For example, the main character of *Wood, Wire, Wings* is Emma Lilian Todd. The main character of *The Fire of Stars* is Cecilia Payne.

Yet the main character doesn't have to be human. In *Bobcat Prowling* by Maria Gianferrari, illustrated by Bagram Ibatoulline, the main character is a yearling, a young bobcat. In *Survivor Tree* by Marcie Colleen, illustrated by Aaron Becker, the main character is a pear tree nearly destroyed on September 11, 2001. In the last chapter, we discussed how *Honeybee* by Candace Fleming, illustrated by Eric Rohmann, is a biography of a bee. I think of my book *A True Wonder*, illustrated by Katy Wu, as a biography of the fictional character Wonder Woman. When selecting a main character, make sure there is something about them a child can identify with. Often it's the lesson the main character is learning.

The Story Goal, Quest, or Problem

In a narrative, the reader's overarching question is "Will the main character achieve their goal?" This basic question is what keeps the reader turning the pages to the end. And that's where the **tension**—and the emotion—lie. The goal has to matter to the main character. It must be something they want more than anything else in the world.

In my favorite book on narrative structure, Blake Snyder's *Save the Cat!*, Snyder says the main character's goal has to be "primal." Take Emma Lilian Todd. She doesn't decide to build an airplane, her big goal, because it seems like a fun thing to do. She makes that choice because she thinks airplanes are the future and she's going to prove a point: a woman can build a far more useful airplane than men can.

In *Bobcat Prowling*, the bobcat yearling's goal is primal: his mother has sent him off to find his own territory where he'll hunt for food.

It's a story about survival. *Survivor Tree* is about survival, too—the tree's whole goal is to survive and thrive in a post-September 11 world.

The goal must be difficult, too. If your character succeeds in reaching their goal on the very first try, you don't have a story. Or at least you don't have a narrative. The struggle is the story. If your research doesn't show that your main character struggled, you need to look at a different structure.

The bottom line is that the main character's goal must be both meaningful to them and difficult to achieve. Together, these two ideas give your book **stakes** and keep the reader turning pages.

A Change

By pursuing their goal, the main character changes from the beginning to the end of the book. This inner change is what's known as a character arc.

The change in the main character should be closely linked to your book's takeaway. The main character learns the takeaway by experiencing the plot events. And because the main character is the reader's avatar, the reader learns the takeaway as well.

Through her struggles and failures, Emma Lilian Todd learns she must fail to succeed. The reader learns that, too. The tree in *Survivor Tree* learns it can survive terrible tragedies; it is resilient. The reader learns the power of resilience, too.

Sometimes the main characters don't change themselves, but they change the world around them. These are known as **flat arc** stories because the main character's arc is flat. In *A True Wonder*, the character of Wonder Woman stays true to who she is throughout the book. However, she changes the world around her, proving that anyone can be a hero, not just the brash and brawny guys of the 1930s and '40s. That's the takeaway.

KEY MOMENTS IN A NARRATIVE

Narratives have predictable moments. In *Save the Cat!*, Blake Snyder outlines fifteen **story beats** that all stories share. However, because picture books are so short, they don't typically have every beat. Here are some of the key story beats picture book narratives typically contain.

Setup: Life Before

What was your character's life like before they got the big idea to pursue their goal? This setup is often just a couple of spreads in the book. A glimpse into the character's life "before" gives us something to compare to the endpoint. That way, we can see how the main character has changed. In biographies, the setup may be a few moments from the main character's childhood. In *A True Wonder*, we see the world of comics before *Wonder Woman* appeared on the scene. In *The Fire of Stars*, we get a glimpse into Cecilia Payne's childhood as a curious girl. In *Survivor Tree*, we see the tree's daily life nestled between the Twin Towers.

Inciting Incident: The Moment Everything Changes

What sends your main character off to pursue their goal? For Emma Lilian Todd, it was seeing some of the early, fantastical airplane designs. She knew she could do better. For Cecilia Payne, it was figuring out a scientific phenomenon all by herself as a girl. That's the moment she fell in love with the thrill of discovery. For the tree in *Survivor Tree*, it was September 11, when it lost its home.

The inciting incident is a critical turning point for the main character. After the inciting incident, life will never be the same. They can't go back to the way things were before. Their only option is to move forward in pursuit of their goal.

Struggles (and Mostly Failures)

Now your main character tries and fails to achieve their goal. Remember, if they achieve their goal or solve their problem on the very first try, you don't have a story. Page-turning tension and learning the takeaway come from trying and failing. Repeatedly.

Picture books are short, so often you see three-ish attempts to solve the problem. And each attempt must logically lead to the next. You can't include anything that isn't advancing the plot. So, for example, I can't have Lilian Todd step away from creating her airplane to start the Junior Aero Club and build kites with schoolboys. This only makes sense if creating the Junior Aero Club somehow directly contributed to creating her airplane (which it didn't, sadly).

One way to test if each attempt logically leads to the next is to try to insert the words "because of that" between each trial and failure. This is something I learned in a lesson on **story spines** from "Pixar in a Box" on Khan Academy.

Here is how this looked for *The Fire of Stars*:

Once upon a time, there was a young girl, Cecilia Payne, who was captivated by the natural world. [setup]

Every day she studied nature all around her. **[setup]**

Until one day, she discovered on her own why a bee orchid looked like a bee, and her whole body hummed with that discovery. In that moment, she decided she wanted to feel like that her whole life. **[inciting incident]**

But Cecilia's family moved to London to find a better school for her brother, and because of that, Cecilia went to a new school with no space for a curious girl like her.

Because of that, she hid out in a secret place: a dusty science lab for older girls.

Because of that, she taught herself about science and soon required a science tutor, who gave Cecilia her first book on astronomy.

Because of that, Cecilia was accepted to Cambridge University to study botany—the next best thing, since women couldn't study astronomy.

Because of that, she took science classes where teachers wanted her to learn facts, not learn anything new. ...

You get the idea. Every plot point must logically lead to the next in a smooth chain of cause and effect. Inserting the words "because of that" helps you test for cause and effect and prevents you from adding fluff that doesn't move the plot forward.

All Is Lost/Dark Night of the Soul: The Lowest Moment

The main character usually experiences a moment of deep despair that causes them to almost give up on their goal. The main character wonders, "Why did I even try this in the first place?! I should have just stayed home." In *Wood, Wire, Wings*, this is the moment when Lilian Todd wheels her airplane out in front of everyone at the Interborough

Fair and the engine just won't work. Talk about humiliating! In *A True Wonder*, the "all is lost" moment is when Wonder Woman's writers take away the superhero's lasso and superpowers and turn her into a Charlie's Angels–type figure.

There are books where the "all is lost" moment is harder to detect. In those books, I look for what I consider the lowest moment. It often comes right before the final success. In *Survivor Tree*, it's when the tree returns to Manhattan but "hesitated to fill the empty sky." In *Bobcat Prowling*, it's the moment when spring comes and the bobcat has wandered so long that he has become an adult. Will he finally find his new territory?

Life After

In the end, your main character succeeds in some way, even if what they accomplish isn't exactly what they set out to do. The main character—and by extension the reader—learns the lesson of the book. Sometimes the last pages of the book even state the takeaway explicitly. That's something I did in *A True Wonder*.

EXERCISE 4: THUMBNAILING A NARRATIVE BOOK

In the next few chapters, you will analyze books' story structures using a process called thumbnailing. Thumbnailing is a lot like storyboarding a movie or TV show. Storyboards consist of words and pictures in boxes that summarize the key scenes in a movie. They look like comic strips and are typically created during the planning process, before movies or TV shows are written.

Picture book writers can use the same technique to summarize their book's major scenes after it is written. It's an easier way to get a big-picture view of what happens in a book and when.

- Start by picking a narrative nonfiction picture book, preferably published in the last five years.
- Download a thumbnail template from author Debbie Ridpath Ohi's website. You'll find the link on the resources page of my website. Or simply draw a series of rectangles in

your writer's notebook. Each rectangle represents two facing pages of the book, called a spread.

- Number the pages on the rectangles. Picture books often start one of two ways: with a single right-hand page, which is page 3. Or they start on a full spread, pages 4 and 5. The title page and publication information appear on the previous pages.
- Going spread by spread, summarize the main idea of each spread in a single sentence. Think about the story moment the spread represents. Is it part of the …
- Setup?
- Inciting incident?
- Struggles and failures?
- "All is lost" moment?
- Life after?
- Then answer the following questions:
- Who is the main character?
- What is the main character's life like before the inciting incident? How many spreads does the author use to set that up?
- What is the inciting incident—the moment everything changes and the main character embarks on their quest? Where does it fall in the book?
- What does the main character want more than anything else in the world?
- How does the main character struggle (and fail)?
- Is there an "all is lost" moment where the main character almost throws in the towel? If not, what's the lowest moment? On what spread does it occur?
- How is the main character's life changed at the end? How does it link to the takeaway?
- Compare and contrast the opening and closing spreads or scenes. What do you notice?
- Would narrative be a good choice for your book? If so, what can you learn from this pattern?

If you go through this process for several nonfiction picture books, you'll start to see patterns. For example, the setup is often brief and the inciting incident happens early in the book. Later in this book, you'll use this knowledge of what's typical to rewrite your own book.

But before you do, let's look at some other story structures—because narrative is just one of many options.

CHAPTER 5
MORE CHRONOLOGICAL STRUCTURE OPTIONS

There's more than one way to tell a story. Narrative structure doesn't make sense for every book. Luckily, there are many other options for organizing examples and events, including several chronological story structures discussed here. Would one of these work for your story?

After reading Chapter 5, you will:

- Know seven more chronological story structures
- Understand the key features of each structure
- Evaluate whether one might work for your story

LIGHTNING STRIKES

In May 2017, I was working on final edits for *The Fire of Stars* so my agent could send it out to publishers. At that time, the book had only one storyline: Cecilia Payne discovering what stars were made of. It used run-of-the-mill narrative structure, just like we discussed in the last chapter. There was nothing wrong with the biography of Cecilia Payne-Gaposchkin. It just wasn't very exciting.

At that time, the market was already tightening for picture book biographies, including women-in-STEM bios. I worried a bit about how easily the book would sell.

Meanwhile, I was working on a blog post with fellow author Hannah Holt for a series called "Query Letters That Worked" on Sub It Club. Holt shared her query for her book *The Diamond and the Boy: The Creation of Diamonds & the Life of H. Tracy Hall*, illustrated by Jay Fleck, which had been acquired by Balzer + Bray and was scheduled to be published the following year.

Reading Holt's **query letter**, two things struck me: Holt pitched her book as a double biography. I'd seen these before, but with two human main characters. What was different about Holt's book was that one of the two main characters was a rock. Secondly, Holt envisioned the boy's story starting from the front of the book and the rock's story starting from the back. The two stories would meet in the middle with a shared phrase.

Holt's query gave me an idea: what if my book could be a double bio, too, with a star as one of the main characters? And what if I pushed Holt's idea further, telling both stories together at the same time with a shared line of text on every spread? It was a huge challenge, but I knew if I could pull it off, I'd have a truly special book.

My agent agreed. By mid-June the revised book was out on **submission**, and six weeks later we had a competitive situation with three editors vying for the story.

This experience taught me the power of unique story structures to help tell—and sell—a story.

WHAT IS A CHRONOLOGICAL STRUCTURE?

Picture the recipe for your favorite chocolate chip cookies. A recipe isn't a narrative. It doesn't have a main character. But your cookie recipe is organized chronologically. First you beat the butter and sugar. Then you add the eggs, followed by flour. Imagine if you tried to bake the cookies before you even added all the ingredients. It would be a mess!

In a recipe, and in chronological story structures, things must happen in a specific order. If you introduce the examples and events out of order, you'll confuse the reader.

Let's look at a few chronological, but not necessarily narrative, structures. (One note: Normally I recommend you study books that have been published in the last five years, since the nonfiction market and what it favors changes rapidly. However, in this section I've included some older books, which I think stand up as model structures.)

Parallel: Two Stories Together

- *Martin & Mahalia: His Words, Her Song* by Andrea Davis Pinkney, illustrated by Brian Pinkney
- *The Diamond and the Boy* by Hannah Holt, illustrated by Jay Fleck
- *The Fire of Stars* by Kirsten W. Larson, illustrated by Katherine Roy

Unlike the rest of the structures we discuss in this chapter, a parallel story is a narrative—it's two narratives interwoven. Most frequently, parallel stories have two human main characters with something in common. The two stories start separately but intersect at some point in time.

For example, in *Martin & Mahalia*, Pinkney introduces the reader to Martin Luther King Jr. and singer Mahalia Jackson on alternating two-page spreads. Pinkney traces each character's journey separately, moving back and forth between them to show how they were both born "with the gift of gospel" even as children. Then she shows how their relationship with the gospel deepened as they grew up, how they both came to know each other's work, and so on. Finally, she shows how the two appeared together at the 1963 March on Washington. Readers will notice lots of repetitive words and phrases between the two narratives, which help underscore the parallels between Martin Luther King Jr. and Mahalia Jackson.

Holt and I took similar approaches with our books. First, we picked inanimate-object main characters closely associated with our human main characters. In *The Diamond and the Boy*, the object is a rock, the object that transforms into a diamond. This is a perfect parallel for Holt's human main character, H. Tracy Hall, the inventor of synthetic diamonds.

In *The Fire of Stars*, how a star forms is the perfect parallel for the formation of Cecilia Payne as a star scientist. Her discovery about what makes the stars helped future scientists figure out how stars form, live, and die.

As in *Martin & Mahalia*, Holt and I used repetitive words and phrases to reinforce the parallels. In *The Fire of Stars*, each spread includes a single line of text that applies to both stories, since the two stories are told simultaneously.

What is the advantage of adding a second narrative with an inanimate object? These stories can appeal to two types of readers: those who love stories about people and those who are fascinated by facts and learning new information.

Cumulative: The House That Jack Built

- *'Ohana Means Family* by Ilima Loomis, illustrated by Kenard Pak
- *The Mess That We Made* by Michelle Lord, illustrated by Julia Blattman
- *The Nest That Wren Built* by Randi Sonenshine, illustrated by Anne Hunter

Cumulative books typically follow the pattern set up in the nursery rhyme "This Is the House That Jack Built":

> *This is the house that Jack built.*
> *This is the malt*
> *that lay in the house that Jack built.*
> *This is the rat,*

that ate the malt
that lay in the house that Jack built.
This is the cat,
that kill'd the rat,
that ate the malt
that lay in the house that Jack built.

You can think of cumulative books as a pyramid. You start with one block of information: "This is the house that Jack built." I've indicated that phrase with the number 1 below. Then subsequent pages add a new block of information and repeat all the blocks that came before. So, the next part of the poem is "This is the malt" (Block 2), and then we repeat Block 1 ("that lay in the house that Jack built"). The third spread adds a third block, "This is the rat," but then repeats Blocks 2 ("that ate the malt") and 1 ("that lay in the house that Jack built.") Visually, it looks like this:

1

21

321

4321

Like other chronological books, the action in cumulative books must happen in a specific order, with one thing leading to the next. These books also typically adopt the rhythmic pattern of "This Is the House That Jack Built."

In *'Ohana Means Family*, Loomis begins, "This is the kalo to make the poi for our 'ohana's lu'au." The next spread adds a second block ("This is the mud") and then repeats Block 1 ("that grows the kalo for our 'ohana's lu'au"). The third spread adds, "This is the water, clear and cold," before repeating Blocks 2 and 1.

As the book progresses, we learn how poi is an accumulation of the Hawaiian people's entire history, culture, and environment.

Lord's *The Mess That We Made* follows a similar structure to show how small choices we've made have accumulated into the Great Pacific Garbage Patch. Cumulative structure might be a good fit for your book if your goal is to show how many small things add up to one big thing.

Cause-and-Effect Structure

- *Because of an Acorn* by Lola M. Schaefer and Adam Schaefer, illustrated by Frann Preston-Gannon
- *If You Take Away the Otter* by Susannah Buhrman-Deever, illustrated by Matthew Trueman
- *If Bees Disappeared* by Lily Williams

Cause-and-effect structure is similar to cumulative structure in many ways. Think of this structure as a chain of dominoes all lined up. You flick the first domino, and the others topple one after another, as each domino hits the next. Visually, it looks like this:

12

23

34

45

For example, in *Because of an Acorn*, we see that because of an acorn (1), an oak tree grows (2). Because of that oak tree (2), a bird nests (3). Because of the bird nesting (3), a seed is dislodged (4). And because a seed is dislodged (4), a flower grows (5). There is some repetition, but unlike cumulative structure, you don't repeat every single line or example that came before.

Some cause-and-effect books, like *If Bees Disappeared*, start with several spreads that provide background information before launching into causes and effects. For example, Williams starts with a discussion of bees as a keystone species before using the cause-and-effect dominoes to show how removing bees from the ecosystem leads from one problem to another.

Buhrman-Deever uses a similar approach in *If You Take Away the Otter*. She uses six spreads to set up how important the ocean's kelp forest is for a variety of species before she explores what happened when otters were hunted almost to extinction. Without otters, their food—the urchins—began to reproduce at alarming speeds. Because the sea urchins reproduced so much, they overate the kelp. Because they overate the kelp, sea creatures lost their homes. Throughout the book, she shows how one change—hunting the otters—rippled through the ecosystem with devastating effects.

As with cumulative structure, cause-and-effect structure can be used for stories that show how one small event or change sets off a chain reaction that ripples and grows with good or bad results.

Circular Structure

- *Flying Deep: Climb Inside Deep-Sea Submersible Alvin* by Michelle Cusolito, illustrated by Nicole Wong
- *Water Is Water* by Miranda Paul, illustrated by Jason Chin
- *No Monkeys, No Chocolate* by Melissa Stewart and Allen Young, illustrated by Nicole Wong

The defining feature of circular books is that they start and end in the same place, perhaps with a slight variation. In other words, they come full circle. The classic fictional example is *If You Give a Mouse a Cookie* by Laura Numeroff, illustrated by Felicia Bond, which starts with the title phrase, "If you give a mouse a cookie, he's going to ask for a glass of milk." If you give him the milk, he'll ask for a straw and then a napkin. This "if/then" pattern continues until the mouse finally realizes he's thirsty again and asks for a glass of milk. And if you give him a glass of milk, he'll ask for a cookie. Numeroff has brought us right back to where we started: giving the mouse a cookie.

In *Water Is Water*, a book about the water cycle, Miranda Paul begins with liquid water. She writes, "Drip. Sip. Pour me a cup. Water is water unless … it heats up" into steam. Then "steam is steam unless it cools high" into clouds. Then "clouds are clouds unless they form low," making fog. The book traces water through its different forms—liquid, gas, liquid again, solid—before ending once more as liquid, this time as apple cider. The end is much like the beginning, with a slight twist: "Drip. Sip, Pour me a cup. Cider is cider … until we drink up!"

In *Flying Deep*, Michelle Cusolito begins with the submersible Alvin above the ocean preparing for its deep-sea mission. Then we follow the submersible and its crew down, down, down to explore the deepest reaches of the ocean. When the mission is complete, they head up, up, up before ending above the surface again. The book begins and ends at the same place: with Alvin on the sea's surface. The slight variation is the time of day—morning versus evening.

Cusolito uses time to mark sections of the story. One of my students brilliantly noted that time is circular, too, just like the face of an old-fashioned analog clock.

In *No Monkeys, No Chocolate*, Melissa Stewart starts with cocoa beans, which come from cocoa pods. Cocoa pods need flowers to form. Flowers need cocoa leaves and midges. Stewart moves backward in time, tracing the whole journey of how cocoa beans are formed and ending right where she started, with cocoa beans. The book starts and ends with cocoa beans and monkeys who help spread them. In a unique twist, the book moves backward in a circle before ending in the same spot.

Circular books are particularly appropriate for books about natural cycles—or any cycle that repeats over and over again. Think life cycles, the water cycle, the rock cycle, and so on.

Reverse Structure

- *Before She Was Harriet* by Lesa Cline-Ransome, illustrated by James E. Ransome

Like other chronological books, reverse books move one way in time—only backward instead of forward. They tell us what came before, as in *No Monkeys, No Chocolate*. It's an unusual structure, as you can tell by the fact that I gave you only one example book.

In *Before She Was Harriet*, the reverse structure is a perfect match for Lesa Cline-Ransome's takeaway: that we can all live many lives, and that heroes aren't necessarily born but made of their experiences.

Think about how many books there are about Harriet Tubman. A lot of them focus on her life as an abolitionist. But Cline-Ransome wants to show us that people can be more than one thing. She wants to show us that we can all lead many lives. Then she shows us who Harriet Tubman was before she became the famous figure we know.

Before She Was Harriet repeats the phrase "before she was" to step us back in time through the many different roles Harriet Tubman played. First an old woman, before that a suffragist, before that a general, before that a Union spy. The book ends at the furthest point back in time: Harriet's childhood.

The key to a successful reverse structure is to avoid jumping around. Move only one way in time. Because this structure can be difficult for young readers to follow, a repeated phrase helps remind the young reader what is happening.

Reverse structure may be a good fit for any story where you want to peel back the layers of an onion to get to the origin or a central idea. You can also think of it like opening a set of Russian nesting dolls.

Problem-Solution Structure

- *Mesmerized: How Ben Franklin Solved a Mystery That Baffled All of France* by Mara Rockliff, illustrated by Iacopo Bruno
- *Mimic Makers: Biomimicry Inventors Inspired by Nature* by Kristen Nordstrom, illustrated by Paul Boston

This will come as no surprise, but problem-solution books have two halves. The first part sets up the problem; the second describes the solution. In *Mesmerized*, Rockliff sets up the book's sole problem in the first eighteen pages of the book. The mysterious Dr. Mesmer is bilking French people out of their money by claiming he has a magical force that can cure everything. Doctors, who are losing patients and money, are outraged. The king's solution? Call in Ben Franklin. Franklin then uses the scientific method to solve the problem and prove Mesmer is a fraud.

Nordstrom's *Mimic Makers* also features a problem-solution structure, but slightly different. She sets up eight different problems, each with their own solution. For example, how do you prevent super-fast bullet trains from making sonic booms? Solution: take inspiration from a bird's beak when creating the design. Problem: How do you make solar cells more lightweight and flexible? Solution: take inspiration from leaves, which harness the sun's energy for their food. Each solution directly follows its problem on alternating spreads.

Problem-solution is a flexible structure that can be used for a variety of stories, from slices of history to technological discoveries.

How-to Structure

- *How to Build an Insect* by Roberta Gibson, illustrated by Anne Lambelet
- *You're Invited to a Moth Ball: A Nighttime Insect Celebration* by Loree Griffin Burns, illustrated by Ellen Harasimowicz

Remember our chocolate chip cookie recipe? Recipes have a how-to structure; they tell readers how to do something step by step. There is a list of ingredients and a process section that describes how to prepare and mix things together. The same goes for how-to book structure.

For example, *How to Build an Insect* takes the reader through the process of building an insect, adding each ingredient one by one. Gibson starts with the head, adds a thorax, then an abdomen. With each step, Gibson asks the reader questions like "How many legs does an insect need?" Each "ingredient" gives her an opportunity to compare and contrast insect and human bodies.

Likewise, *You're Invited to a Moth Ball* lays out the process for putting together a nighttime moth-viewing party. Burns describes what you need (the "ingredients"): a rope, a UV light, an extension cord, etc. Then she moves on to how to set things up ("the process"), so the moths will attend the party.

Why should an author consider how-to structure? It gets your reader actively involved in the story. In fact, author Melissa Stewart calls this type of nonfiction "active nonfiction" in her book *5 Kinds of Nonfiction*. This structure is often used for cookbooks, coding books, craft books, and the like, where kids are engaged in making something or completing activities. Authors have adapted the structure to add interactivity to informational books.

EXERCISE 5: STUDYING CHRONOLOGICAL STRUCTURE

Pick a mentor text that uses a chronological structure, preferably published in the last five years. You may choose from parallel narrative, cumulative, circular, reverse, cause and effect, problem-solution, or how-to. I keep Pinterest boards of books organized by various structures, which you'll find linked on my website.

Follow the same process you used in the last chapter to thumbnail the mentor text. You may use Debbie Ridpath Ohi's templates or draw your own thumbnails in your notebook. Summarize the main idea of each spread in one line per rectangle and note how each spread helps the story unfold. Then answer these questions:

- What are some things you noticed by thumbnailing this book?
- What work does the first spread do?
- What work does the last spread do?
- How are examples ordered?
- Do kids appear in this book? If not, how does this text connect with the child reader? What's its kid appeal?
- What are some learnings you can apply to your work in progress?
- If you are using a chronological structure now, is the current structure working?

- If not, what shifts might you need to make based on your mentor text analysis?
- If you are not using one of these chronological structures, could one of them work for your story? Why or why not?

If you don't think any of these structures is a fit for your story, don't despair. The next chapter includes more options for structuring your nonfiction picture book.

NONCHRONOLOGICAL STORY SHAPES

Following a chronology isn't the only way to tell a story. In fact, one of the most popular structures for all nonfiction books—description text structure—doesn't follow a chronology at all. Still, books without a chronological structure require some level of organization. Let's look at some options.

After reading Chapter 6, you will:

- Have a thorough understanding of four nonchronological story structures
- Understand the key features of each
- Know whether they might be a fit for your story

DESCRIPTION STRUCTURE

- *Glitter Everywhere!: Where It Came From, Where It's Found & Where It's Going* by Chris Barton, illustrated by Chaaya Prabhat
- *Tiny Creatures: The World of Microbes* by Nicola Davies, illustrated by Emily Sutton
- *Grand Canyon* by Jason Chin

Rather than give readers a slice of a specific topic, books with a description structure aim to provide a broad overview of the topic. These books explain the topic's key features and/or explain how the topic works. With every spread, the author considers what readers need to know and when they need to know it. Each new idea logically builds on what's come before to expand the reader's knowledge.

According to the publisher, *Glitter Everywhere!* covers "the good, the bad, and shiny of all things glitter." If you can call a book an "all things" book or an "all about" book, that's a big hint it might use a description structure.

So how does Barton organize his information and examples? He starts with a definition of iridescence and how it is found in nature, citing mica and beetles as examples. He discusses how glitter came to be used in human celebrations, then turns to the invention of plastic glitter and how it rose in popularity, before finally discussing the environmental impacts. By the time the reader closes the book, they feel they know all about glitter.

Likewise, in *Tiny Creatures*, Davies introduces microbes, what they are, and where they live. She also covers how they are shaped, what they eat (and how they eat), how they transform food scraps into compost and milk into yogurt, how they reproduce, and how certain types can make you sick. She also shows how other microbes are helpful, doing big things. The idea that small things can do big jobs is Davies's takeaway. To reinforce the idea, she starts her book with how tiny microbes are and ends with their big jobs, helping readers transform their thinking and assumptions about microbes.

Jason Chin's *Grand Canyon* covers every aspect of the Grand Canyon, from where it's located, to how it formed, to the plants and animals that live there. His descriptive text is organized by elevation, starting at the Inner Gorge, in the deepest point of the canyon, and moving upward, following a girl and her dad as they hike out of the canyon.

Internet and encyclopedia articles use a description structure. That means the information contained in a book with a descriptive structure probably is readily available at kids' fingertips. To make a description book worthy of being published by a large publisher, some other aspect of the book must be truly special. For example, the fact that Barton's book is the first ever on the topic of glitter, an object with mass kid appeal, sets it apart. Illustrations are another differentiating factor for these books. Author/illustrators frequently create nonfiction books with descriptive structures. A strong takeaway, like the one found in Nicola Davies's *Tiny Creatures*, helps, too.

LIST STRUCTURE

- *Plants Can't Sit Still* by Rebecca E. Hirsch, illustrated by Mia Posada
- *We Are Still Here!: Native American Truths Everyone Should Know* by Traci Sorell, illustrated by Frané Lessac
- *No Voice Too Small: Fourteen Young Americans Making History* edited by Lindsay H. Metcalf, Keila V. Dawson, and Jeanette Bradley; illustrated by Jeanette Bradley
- *Jazz Day: The Making of a Famous Photograph* by Roxane Orgill, illustrated by Francis Vallejo

List books are incredibly popular, and there are many different variations on the structure. Traditionally, authors used list structure to tell stories about the animal and natural world, but increasingly they have adopted it for histories and collective biographies, making list structure quite flexible.

In a list book, the first spread often explains the author's takeaway or premise, especially if the concept isn't explained by the title. For example, in *Plants Can't Sit Still*, Hirsch tells readers on page 1 that plants can move in many ways. Subsequent spreads provide a list of examples to prove her point, from seedlings worming their way out of the soil, to dandelion fluff blowing in the wind, to coconuts bobbing on waves to find a new home. The final spread reinforces the takeaway again, returning to the idea of plants moving in many ways.

In the absence of a narrative or other chronological structure, authors using a list structure have to cleverly organize their examples for maximum tension and page turn. For example, Hirsch's examples move from the simple and familiar (seeds squirming) to the surprising ways plants move (coconuts floating on oceans). She moves through a cycle of first day, then night. The passing of time is shown in the illustrations. And Hirsch starts and ends with seeds, following the plant life cycle and giving the book a circular ending that points back to the beginning.

As I mentioned earlier, though list structure is very common in books about the natural world, authors now use it for history and even biography. Sorell's *We Are Still Here!* is a list book. The takeaway is that we haven't closed the book on Native Americans and their history. They are literally still here. Sorell doesn't explain the takeaway on the first spread, especially since it's in the title. Rather she leaves it to Frané Lessac's illustrations. Lessac sets up the book by showing families arriving at a Native American school for Indigenous Peoples' Day. The school's children have prepared presentations about aspects of their people's history. The student Wenona presents assimilation, Kee's presentation is about allotment, etc. These topics form Sorell's supporting examples.

Collective biographies also can use a list structure. In *No Voice Too Small*, an opening poem tells readers that no voice is too small to solve a big problem. Each example is a mini-biography of a young American working to make big changes by combating bullying, climate change, etc. The final poem reinforces the takeaway: that we can all make change. *Muslim Girls Rise: Inspirational Champions of Our Time* by Saira Mir, illustrated by Aaliya Jaleel, uses a similar structure; it's a list of biographies of Muslim women doing amazing things in every career field.

Finally, *Jazz Day* uses a list structure to discuss the story behind a famous 1958 photograph of jazz musicians that appeared in *Esquire Magazine*. In a sense, it's a series of mini-biographies, but they are organized around a single moment in time—how the photograph came to be—versus a specific idea like child activism in *No Voice Too Small*. Orgill writes a prologue to set up the idea and then includes a poem about each person who appears in the photograph. The final three poems capture the moment the photographer, Art Kane, takes the shot and, later, one of the boys from the magazine seeing himself in the published photo. The last poem praises Art Kane.

List books seem simple, but they can be sneakily complex. Often, authors must add layers of organization to make their books surprising and keep readers turning pages. Books using list structure require strong takeaways or concepts and a vivid voice, which we'll discuss in upcoming chapters. Still, this structure is also flexible and can be used for many stories.

COMPARE-AND-CONTRAST STRUCTURE

- *Birds of a Feather: Bowerbirds and Me* by Susan L. Roth
- *Lincoln and Kennedy: A Pair to Compare* by Gene Barretta
- *Freaky, Funky Fish: Odd Facts about Fascinating Fish* by Debra Kempf Shumaker, illustrated by Claire Powell
- *Fourteen Monkeys: A Rainforest Rhyme* by Melissa Stewart, illustrated by Steve Jenkins

Books with a compare-and-contrast structure look at two or more elements and discuss how they are alike and different. Some compare-and-contrast books compare just two things. In *Birds of a Feather*, Susan L. Roth compares and contrasts humans and bowerbirds to show how we are alike, or "birds of a feather."

In *Lincoln and Kennedy*, the focus is only on those two presidents, examining their childhoods, their families, and their major challenges as presidents. What sets these compare-and-contrast books apart from parallel books like *The Fire of Stars* is the absence of a narrative arc. There is no inciting incident, no struggles and failures, and no change from beginning to end. Each spread simply discusses the ways two people or objects are the same and different.

Other compare-and-contrast books use several examples to make their point. In *Freaky, Funky Fish,* Shumaker compares and contrasts more than eighteen fish to prove her point that fish aren't boring, but freaky and funky. In *Fourteen Monkeys*, Melissa Stewart's title says it all. She compares and contrasts fourteen rainforest monkey species to show the different ways they have all adapted to survive in the same habitat.

In compare-and-contrast books, the first spread often explains the takeaway if the title didn't capture it. Each subsequent spread (or couple of spreads) provides supporting examples, drawing comparisons and highlighting differences. As with list books, there is often another level of organization layered in or another element that pulls readers through the story. In *Fourteen Monkeys*, the book follows a day/night cycle. In *Freaky, Funky Fish*, the rhyme pulls the reader through the book. And, as with list books, compare-and-contrast endings often reinforce the takeaway and connect the idea to the reader in some way.

What can you compare and contrast? Almost anything from people to animals and inanimate objects. Like list structure, compare-and-contrast structure is flexible.

QUESTION-AND-ANSWER STRUCTURE

- *Bone by Bone: Comparing Animal Skeletons* by Sara Levine, illustrated by T. S. Spookytooth
- *Whose Hands Are These?: A Community Helper Guessing Book* by Miranda Paul, illustrated by Luciana Navarro Powell
- *Meow!: The Truth about Cats* by Annette Whipple

What's the organizing principle in a question-and-answer (Q&A) book? Questions and answers. Asking a series of rhetorical questions and providing answers is what pulls the reader through the book, often giving a "guessing game" feel to the text, especially if the question is asked on one spread and then answered on the next. When questions are asked and answered on different pages, it builds anticipation for the reader and encourages them to turn the page.

That's what Sara Levine does masterfully in *Bone by Bone*. She asks the reader what would happen if their bones grew or shrunk, or were added to or subtracted from. Readers must turn the page to see what would happen and to learn about an animal that has each type of skeleton described.

The same is true of *Whose Hands Are These?* Each spread includes a short poem about a community helper and how they use their hands. The community helper isn't named. Paul asks, "Whose hands are these?" Readers must turn the page for the answer. In this way, question-and-answer books can make a story interactive for the reader.

In *Meow!*, Annette Whipple uses questions and answers differently. Each spread has a question about cats, which is answered on the same page. In Whipple's book, the rhetorical questions stand in for the child's curiosity and wonderings. Each question Whipple presents is one kids would naturally have. This heightens the reader's curiosity, interest, and satisfaction as they read.

Like other non-narrative books, the opening and closing spreads of a question-and-answer book often capture the author's takeaway and set up the rules of the game. The questions and answers in between provide supporting evidence and examples.

OTHER OPTIONS

At this point you've learned just how many story structure options you have to choose from. But I don't want my examples to constrain you. Instead, I want you to realize the sky's the limit when it comes to story structures. For example, what's the structure of Kate Messner's unusual book, *The Next President*, illustrated by Adam Rex? I don't know! I might call the structure "overlapping." I've never seen another book like it. Moving chronologically, Messner selects certain dates and then provides a snapshot of each living future president, including how old they were on that date and what was happening in their life. She uses this unique framework to inspire kids to think about the potential future presidents among them and what they might be doing right now.

What about *The Important Thing about Margaret Wise Brown* by Mac Barnett, illustrated by Sarah Jacoby? It's a biography, but it doesn't use a narrative or list structure. Instead, it follows the structure of Margaret Wise Brown's *The Important Book* and becomes a rumination about what makes a life important. Meanwhile, a book called *Write to Me: Letters from Japanese American Children to the Librarian They Left Behind* by Cynthia Grady, illustrated by Amiko Hirao, has an epistolary (letter) element to its structure.

I'm less concerned about labels. In fact, I've only labeled the story structures in the last few chapters so you can notice the patterns these different books follow. What's more important is developing your own skill at analyzing a book's structure to see how it's working and to ask big-picture questions: How is the book set up? How are the evidence and examples served on each spread? How are they organized for maximum effect? And of course, I'm most concerned about what possibilities these structures can unlock for your own book.

Breaking a book into chunks by thumbnailing and summarizing the main idea on each spread will help you understand how these books work, no matter their structure. Let's thumbnail one more time.

EXERCISE 6: THUMBNAILING A NONCHRONOLOGICAL BOOK

Pick a mentor text, preferably published within the last five years, that uses a nonchronological structure, whether description, list, compare and contrast, or question and answer. Remember that you can find examples on my Pinterest boards linked on the resources page of my website.

Thumbnail the mentor text using Debbie Ridpath Ohi's templates or by drawing your own rectangles. Summarize the main idea of each spread in one or two lines per rectangle and note how each spread helps the story unfold. Then answer these questions:

- What are some things you noticed after thumbnailing this book?
- What work does the first spread do?
- What work does the last spread do?
- How are examples ordered?
- Do kids appear in this book? If not, how does this text connect with the child reader? What's its kid appeal?
- What are some learnings you can apply to your work in progress?
- For your own book, are you using a nonchronological structure? If so, how is it working?

- If not, what shifts might you need to make based on your mentor text analysis?
- If you are not using one of these nonchronological structures, could one of them work for your story? Why or why not?

CHAPTER 7
THE STRUCTURE REWRITE

You've learned a lot about story structure over the last few chapters. Now it's time to put your new knowledge to work. Revising is all about rewriting.

Throughout this book, you will undertake three major rewrites and then do a bit of tweaking and polishing. This chapter focuses on the first of the three major rewrites: the structure rewrite. In this rewrite, you will either rework the existing structure of your book or try out a completely new one.

Why start with structure? There's no point in tweaking individual scenes or sentences before you get your overall structure right. That would be like wallpapering a room when you need to tear out the walls because your house's structure is all wonky. Always start with the big picture and then work your way to smaller and smaller issues. Throughout this book, you will revise first at the structural level, then at the scene level and the line level (voice), before fine-tuning individual spreads.

After reading Chapter 7, you will:

- Select a structure to try out on your story
- Evaluate secondary structures

- Rewrite your book using a new and/or stronger structure

SELECTING A STRUCTURE

In the most magical picture books, there is a strong connection between the topic, the takeaway, and the structure. For example, Michelle Lord's *The Mess That We Made*—a story about accumulating ocean trash—uses cumulative structure. Brilliant! A circular structure is the perfect choice for *Water Is Water*, Miranda Paul's book about the water cycle. In her series *If Animals Disappeared*, Lily Williams's takeaway is that small choices and changes have big impacts, so cause-and-effect structure is a great fit.

And in *The Fire of Stars*, pairing and paralleling the stories of Cecilia Payne and a star made a lot of sense. My takeaway was how a star is born, both literally and figuratively. In all the books I've mentioned, the form (structure) follows the book's function (topic and takeaway).

LAYERS OF ORGANIZATION

Many of the books you've studied use more than one layer to organize examples and evidence. These additional layers can add to a book's usefulness by providing classroom or educational tie-ins. Remember, the best books can be used multiple ways in the classroom, library, or at home.

For example, Marcie Colleen's *Survivor Tree*, the tale of the pear tree that survived September 11, has a narrative structure. In most cases, teachers or parents would buy it to read in conjunction with the anniversary of September 11. But the book also is organized according to the seasons, moving through the cycle more than once and highlighting the seasonal changes in both the text and the art. Teachers and parents could use the book to teach younger children about the seasons.

Wood, Wire, Wings, my book about airplane inventor Lilian Todd, uses a narrative structure and employs another layer as well. The book follows the engineering design process as taught through the Next Generation Science Standards: defining the problem, brainstorming solutions, and optimizing the design (testing, tweaking, testing again). That means the book teaches not just U.S. history, but also engineering design in the science curriculum.

In *Mesmerized*, Mara Rockliff has done something similar. Her book uses a problem-solution structure. During the solution section of the book, Ben Franklin follows the scientific method, which serves as a secondary structure that makes the book a useful teaching tool for science lessons.

As you pick a structure to explore, you might consider if your book requires a secondary layer of organization. Check the resources section for links to classroom curricula.

EXERCISE 7: STRUCTURE BRAINSTORM

Go back to the spot in your writer's notebook where you journaled about your story spark and your takeaway. Consider:

- Does your topic or takeaway naturally lend itself to a specific structure? If so, which one?
- Brainstorm two or three structures that might work for your story and jot them down in your notebook. If you think your current structure is working well, you can add it to the list of potential structures with a goal of improving it.
- Sit with your potential structures for a bit. Does one of them excite you or fill you with possibilities more than the others? That could be a sign that you should try it out first. When I hit on the parallel structure for *The Fire of Stars*, it was magical. I couldn't wait to sit down and rewrite the story even though I knew it would be difficult.
- Does the prospect of writing a story using any of these structures fill you with dread?
- Listen to your gut and your instincts as you pick a structure to try out. As a writer, it's important to listen to yourself. You likely have a feeling about what your story needs.
  Remember, my goal is to help you tell the story you envision in the best way you can.

- Is there a natural secondary layer of organization that might help your story, like the changing seasons, the transition from day to night, or the engineering design process?

REVISING WITH A BLANK PAGE

This is the tried-and-true process I use to revise every book I write, including *The Fire of Stars*.

1. Thumbnail Mentor Texts

Go to the library and check out as many books as you can that use your chosen structure. Remember, I've curated Pinterest boards with several examples; you'll find them linked on the resources page of my website.

For *The Fire of Stars*, this process meant checking out parallel biography books like *Bird & Diz* by Gary Golio, illustrated by Ed Young, and *Martin & Mahalia*, since Hannah Holt's *The Diamond and the Boy* hadn't been published yet.

Next, print out Debbie Ridpath Ohi's templates or draw a series of rectangles in your notebook. Each rectangle represents a two-page spread in the book.

Read your mentor texts. Summarize the main idea of each spread and write it on the rectangle. Consider what function each spread performs. Is it setup? Inciting incident? Takeaway? Supporting example? Struggle and failure? Cause and effect? As you work through your book pile, do you notice patterns about where these key moments are happening in the majority of the books?

2. Thumbnail Your Book

Now print out another set of Debbie Ridpath Ohi's templates or draw a new series of rectangles. Thumbnail your book, using the mentor texts as a road map. If the mentor texts used two spreads to set up the book's concept or story, give yourself two spreads for the setup. If the inciting incident was on spread 3 in the mentor texts, that's where yours is going. Summarize the main idea from your manuscript that will appear on each page. When you are finished, your thumbnails will serve as your outline.

Just for your amusement, here are some of the thumbnails for *The Fire of Stars* from my author's notebook.

3. Just Write It

Open a blank page in your notebook or on your computer—however you prefer to draft.

You are not allowed to open your previous drafts while rewriting. You are only allowed to refer to your thumbnail outline. Here's why: the minute you open your old drafts, you will get sucked into your old ways of thinking about your story. To successfully rewrite your draft, you will need to leave those old thoughts behind.

You have internalized your story, its events, and its examples over months, maybe even years. You have lived and breathed this story. You know it by heart. Now allow the most important examples and events to bubble up. They will only do that if you keep your old drafts closed.

4. Keep It Short

While you shouldn't worry about word count right now, it's important to have an idea of how much text typically appears on a picture book page. Most two-page spreads have 50 to 100 words. Yes, there are occasional text-heavy books like *Jumbo: The Making of the Boeing 747* by Chris Gall with 200 words on a spread, but in general, too much text leaves little room for the illustrations. Keep this in mind as you rewrite your draft in spread-sized chunks.

5. Give Yourself Permission to Do a Crappy Job

Just get the ideas down on the page. You are only trying to find the shape of your story. We will refine your language—add that wallpaper—in the coming chapters. My favorite quote from author Shannon Hale is appropriate here: "I'm writing a first draft and reminding myself that I'm simply shoveling sand into a box so that later I can build castles."

6. Give Yourself a Time Limit (or All the Time You Need)

Some writers find it helpful to redraft in sprints. If you are one of these writers, give yourself a time limit, say one twenty-five-minute block or two blocks with a break in between, if needed. Close out all distractions (email, social media, children), set a timer, and just go for it. And of course, reward yourself when you are done with a piece of chocolate, a walk, or a new book.

Alternatively, some people find it more helpful to break down this process into smaller chunks, setting a goal of turning one thumbnail into one spread of text each day. Since most picture books are twelve to fifteen spreads, that means it will take you twelve to fifteen days to complete this exercise. Do what works best for you.

7. Forget the Facts and Focus on the Feelings

Do not look at your research. For this draft, it's unimportant whether the grass was green or brown that fall day. Research is a rabbit hole. If you stop drafting to look up one fact, soon you'll be jumping from this book to that book to the internet. Being a stickler for facts at this stage slows you down and can cause you to lose the emotion and shape of your story.

Instead, insert placeholders with a note for any research you need to look up later. I put notes in brackets with three Xs in the front so I can easily search for them in the draft afterward. It looks something like this:

Lilian's plane soared. [XXX check flying speed]

Lilian grew up in [XXX verify birthplace] at a time when everyone was tinkering.

8. If You Get Stuck ...

Try writing your pitch like you would in a query letter. Writing a pitch forces you to distill the essence of your story into a few short sentences that explain what the story is and why a reader (or editor or agent) should care.

As an example, here is the **pitch** from my original *Wood, Wire, Wings* query letter:

Even as a young girl, Emma Lilian Todd itched to transform tin, wire, and wood into her own inventions. When Lilian sees a crow circling overhead one day, she hatches a plan to build a bird-like airplane. In a time when men—and only men—are still learning the science of flight, Lilian hitches up her skirts and rolls up her sleeves, overcoming constant crashes and engine trouble until her airplane—and her dreams—soar.

This pitch shows the setup (Lilian's girlhood) and the inciting incident (seeing the crow fly). It also gives a sense of Lilian's struggles and failures (constant crashes, engine trouble) and the takeaway (perseverance). It encapsulates the entire shape of the story.

If you are stuck, it can be helpful to write the pitch first and then expand it into a full outline or set of thumbnails. Then you can write the whole thing.

For more help with writing pitches, see Blake Snyder's discussion of pitches and loglines in *Save the Cat!*.

When you are finished with your structure rewrite, come back here.

All finished? Woo-hoo!

You've accomplished something incredible. Note this milestone in your writer's notebook or on your calendar so you can track your progress. You have come a lot further than most writers. And that means we're ready for Part 3, where we begin to finesse your story.

SECTION 3: SCENE WRITING

CHAPTER 8
MAKE A SCENE

n *Tell It Like It Is*, author Roy Peter Clark summarizes what a story is: **"The purpose of a story is not to convey information but to capture an experience."** Readers pick up a book not just to learn information but to experience events and examples in real time. They want to be immersed in the story as it unfolds. If readers wanted a simple summary of what happened after the fact, they would read the encyclopedia.

How do we bring readers into the book? By writing in scenes. That's what this section is all about.

After reading Chapter 8, you will:

- Understand scenes versus summaries
- Know the three basic building blocks of a scene (physical action, **internalization**, speech)
- Understand two key features of a scene (sensory details and vivid verbs)
- Know what parts of your story are best suited for scenes
- Conduct a scene analysis
- Craft your own scene

Let's look at the two paragraphs below:

Paragraph 1: Another day [Lilian] took apart the clock, spreading the pieces before her. Did this wheel fit here? Did that lever fit there? She put the pieces back this way. No tick. She put the pieces back that way. No tock. The clock stayed still. Failure! Lilian stood baffled but buoyed by the challenge. [53 words]

Paragraph 2: Even as a schoolgirl, Lilian had a mind for machines. She took apart clocks and typewriters and put them back together ... most of the time. [25 words]

Now pull out your writer's notebook and answer the following questions:

- What key differences do you notice between the two paragraphs?
- Which paragraph is more exciting to read? Why?

Here are some things you may have observed:

- Paragraph 1 is twice as long as Paragraph 2.
- Paragraph 2 tells us what happened after the fact.
- Paragraph 1 shows us what is happening in real time. We experience taking apart the clock alongside Lilian.
- In Paragraph 1, we are in Lilian's head. The rhetorical questions seem to be her thoughts. So does the exclamation, "Failure!"
- There is more tension in Paragraph 1 as we wonder if Lilian will succeed and then how she'll respond when she fails. Will she give up?

THE SCENE: A DEFINITION

Paragraph 2 is an after-the-fact summary, while Paragraph 1 is a scene. If you have ever written a novel, then you have written a scene. But you may not have considered that writing nonfiction requires writing in scenes, too.

In *Scene & Structure*, John Bickham defines a scene as "action unfolding in real time, minute-by-minute in a single time and place."

The key difference between a scene (like Paragraph 1) and a summary (like Paragraph 2) is that idea of minute-by-minute action. In a scene, the reader experiences the action, watching it unfold as if it were playing out on a stage. Like the character, the reader has no idea how the scene will end. That suspense is what keeps the reader reading, creating tension.

Let's look at another scene/summary comparison, and then we'll break down the components of a scene.

A SECOND EXAMPLE

Here's a scene I made up for our purposes. Let's pretend it's from an expository book about animal migration:

Paragraph 3: A cool wind blows in from the north, and the sun dips lower in the sky. It's time to go. The first wing flutters. Then another. A swarm of butterflies flaps, then flies, a whirring blur of orange. Where will they go? Oyamel trees thousands of miles away in Mexico. They must snuggle up before winter arrives. [59 words]

Paragraph 4: Each fall, monarch butterflies migrate to Central Mexico to overwinter. [10 words]

What differences do you notice? Which is more exciting to read and why?

Rich scenes, like Paragraph 3, play like mini-movies in the reader's mind. In fact, when I wrote Paragraph 3, I first pictured it as a nature documentary about butterfly migration. Then I imagined a voiceover (like BBC presenter David Attenborough) narrating the play-by-play action. That voiceover is what I wrote for my scene.

BUILDING BLOCKS OF A SCENE

Scenes have three major building blocks:

- Physical action
- Internalization (emotional reactions and thoughts)
- Speech

Physical action is anything that "plays" on a movie or stage. In Paragraph 1, physical actions include Lilian taking apart the clock, spreading the pieces out before her, and then trying the levers. In Paragraph 3, physical actions include the wind blowing, the sun dipping, and the butterfly wings fluttering. Physical actions also include physical responses like facial expressions and shoulder shrugs. Wincing and smirking are physical actions, too, even though they convey emotion.

Internalization is your character's internal emotional reactions and thoughts. This component doesn't play on a stage or movie screen, so you can't see it. Thoughts and emotions must be stated explicitly or implied through physical responses. In Paragraph 1, the exclamation, "Failure!" suggests Lilian Todd's internal response to the fact that she couldn't get the clock to work. The sentence "Lilian stood baffled but buoyed by the challenge" also captures her internal thoughts. You can't see "baffled" and "buoyed." I had to explicitly tell you her thoughts.

Speech is less common in nonfiction picture books because you can't make up quotes in nonfiction. Every snippet of dialogue must come from documented sources. Only rarely will you find dialogue in a scene, but when you do, it must be authentic.

INTERNALIZATION CONNECTS THE DOTS

Internalization is critical for scene writing, especially in narratives featuring a main character. Internalization reveals a person's character and shows how your protagonist operates and why they make certain choices and act the way they do. In other words, internalization reveals motive.

Look back at Paragraph 1. How would most people react to failure? They might give up and walk away. Others might keep working but grow frustrated. Not Lilian. She is excited and energized by challenges. Her internalization in this scene reveals her relationship to challenges and failure even as a young girl.

Let's contrast Lilian's scene with one that lacks internalization:

> "The votes are in, and Sunghee will be our next class president," Miss Mann said.
>
> Sunghee flinched. He raced from the room.

What is happening here? Sunghee's reaction doesn't make sense without his internalization. Presumably Sunghee ran for class president, so he should be overjoyed by his election. Why is he reacting by flinching and racing from the room? Let's look at some possible internalizations that answer the question "Why?"

> "The votes are in, and Sunghee will be our next class president," Miss Mann said.
>
> Sunghee flinched. Miss Mann had just assigned a huge class project that would take the whole semester. How would Sunghee have enough time for his presidential duties?
>
> He raced from the room.

OR

"The votes are in, and Sunghee will be our next class president," Miss Mann said.

Sunghee flinched. How could this have happened? He'd won against Lourdes, his best friend! He'd only entered the race to pull a few votes away from Boris. Now Lourdes was going to kill him.

He raced from the room.

These two paragraphs reveal something different about Sunghee's character and motivations. In the first, we realize he is a diligent and stressed-out student. In the second, we see a kid whose focus is on being a good friend. In each case, the internalization explains why Sunghee logically might react by racing from the room.

SCENE COMPONENTS IN BOOKS WITHOUT HUMAN MAIN CHARACTERS

In nonfiction, we have to be careful about personification, the process of giving nonhuman characters human characteristics. If the planet Pluto or a flower speaks or has explicit thoughts, a book is no longer nonfiction. It becomes **informational fiction**.

Yet, with nonhuman main characters, we still must connect the dots for the reader. Look again at Paragraph 3 about the butterflies from our expository migration book:

Paragraph 3: A cool wind blows in from the north, and the sun dips lower in the sky. It's time to go. The first wing flutters. Then another. A swarm of butterflies flaps, then flies, a whirring blur of orange. Where will they go? Oyamel trees thousands of miles away in Mexico. They must snuggle up before winter arrives.

The paragraph starts with two actions—the wind blowing and the sun's position—which signal to the butterflies that it's time to migrate. In a sense, "it's time to go" explains the butterflies' instincts, an internal process, without personifying them.

Imagine if I had said, "The butterflies think to themselves, 'It's time to go.'" Now I've given the butterflies explicit human-like thoughts. That's personification—and a no-no.

Next, look at the rhetorical question "Where will they go?" That's a question for the reader, to inspire their own internal wonderings, inviting them into the world of the story. Like the previous phrase, it takes the place of the butterflies' internalization.

If I had been more explicit, this passage would have moved into the realm of informational fiction. For example, if I had written, "The butterflies wonder where they will go," I would have made it very plain these were the butterflies' thoughts. Again, that's personification.

The key with all nonfiction, especially books featuring nonhuman main characters, is to use rhetorical questions and exclamations as necessary to create tension and emotion. The reader's thoughts, emotions, and wonderings stand in for those of the nonhuman characters.

Physical action, internalization, and speech are the three major components of an effective scene. But all scenes, especially scenes with nonhuman characters, require two more components, which I detail below.

SENSORY DETAILS AND VIVID VERBS

Sensory details and vivid verbs are critical for putting readers in the scene, especially in science and nature stories where you may not have a main character.

Sensory details not only reveal what the main character (or the reader) sees, but also what they hear, smell, taste, and feel through touch. Humans tend to be very visual, so we often write with visual details in mind. But for rich scenes, we can't neglect the other senses. Also, because picture books are illustrated, readers will see a picture on the page, capturing visual details. Your words must spark different senses.

In the Paragraph 1 scene featuring Lilian Todd, I wrote "no tick" and "no tock." Those are auditory details—what Lilian (and by extension the reader) is listening for. In Paragraph 3 from the expository book on animal migration, I wrote, "… a cold wind blows." This is something the butterflies and the reader could feel physically. The word "whirring" also conveys what the swarm of butterflies might sound like if the reader were standing right there witnessing the scene.

Strong writing also requires **vivid verbs**. For example, I wrote the butterflies "snuggle up" in the oyamel trees. This is so much stronger than something like "roost close together," which requires both a verb ("roost") and a descriptive phrase ("close together"). "Snuggle" says it all with a single verb, and it's childlike. Don't tell me your main character "ran quickly." Tell me they "sprinted."

NOT EVERYTHING CAN BE A SCENE

Scenes take up a lot of space in your manuscript. Remember my Lilian Todd example? The scene ran 53 words, while the summary was only 25. We can't write every bit of our stories in scene. We must choose the most pivotal moments for scene treatment, especially when writing a narrative. The portions you choose to write in scene should be key moments of struggle and change for your protagonist. These include:

- Major moments that reveal character or motivation
- The inciting incident: the moment your story really gets going and your character sets off to pursue their big goal
- Some of the major struggles and failures, especially your character's response when they don't succeed, so we understand the next choice they make
- The "all is lost" or lowest moment
- Big success: your character's final moment
- Supporting examples in expository books, which are often written in scene or at least with sensory details and vivid verbs

Summary is great for transitions or for covering long time periods. Summary is also good for brief context or backstory we don't need to linger on. For example, in *Wood, Wire, Wings*, I summarized the major breakthroughs in aviation, like the Wright brothers' first flight. These events were context and backstory, and were happening outside of Lilian's experience. She only learned of them after the fact. I wrote, "While Lilian tinkered and tested, other inventors flew the first full-sized airplanes. But when she read the news, she simply shook her head. Their designs still seemed fantastical—not practical."

Meanwhile, Tracy Subisak's illustrations showed what these inventions looked like. Summarizing allowed me to keep the focus on Lilian, my main character, and cover a large time period quickly.

For expository books, especially those with list, compare-and-contrast, or question-and-answer structure, authors often use summary for the opening and closing spreads. These are the spreads where the author is setting up their argument (at the beginning), which the book's examples will support, and then drawing conclusions (at the end).

EXERCISE 8: SCENE BREAKDOWN

Grab a favorite nonfiction picture book off your shelf and locate a moment where the action is unfolding minute by minute. In other words, choose a scene, not a summary. Then look for evidence of the following:

- Physical action (especially unfolding in real time)
- Internalization (internal thoughts and emotions, either explicitly stated or suggested)
- Speech
- Sensory details that speak to all five senses—what we can see, hear, touch, taste, and smell
- Vivid verbs

Then analyze the scene's effect. Do you feel like you are there? What emotional response does the scene evoke for you?

EXERCISE 9: REWRITE A SCENE

Go back to your current manuscript and highlight a moment that should be written in scene but isn't. Using what you've learned in this chapter, rewrite the passage as a scene using the basic scene building blocks as well as sensory details and vivid verbs. You will need to mine your research for many of these details, so don't be surprised if writing your scene takes a while.

Advice for Writing Scenes

When you draft a scene:

- Imagine you are narrating a nature documentary or a movie.
- Picture it in your mind and narrate what you see happening moment by moment. As a commentator, you must explain to the audience why the person or animal does what they do. This "why" will become the internalization.
- If it's easier, you can even turn on a voice recording in a program like Google Docs and narrate out loud, allowing the word-processing program to turn your speech into text.
- If you are having a hard time, write in present tense and then convert the scene to past tense later.
- If you are distracted by a particular piece of research, just put [XXX] as a placeholder for the research and keep writing your scene. You can consult your research for those details later.

CHAPTER 9
SCENE TEST

Scenes are a series of causes and effects. They also raise and answer questions for the reader and contribute to the overall arc of your story. Learning to test your scenes for each of these components is critical to writing successful scenes.

After reading Chapter 9, you will:

- Understand cause and effect in a scene
- Identify missing causes or effects
- Be able to pinpoint when causes and effects are out of order
- Understand the natural order of the scene building blocks
- Learn the perils of filter words and creative dialogue tags
- Evaluate your own scene for these elements
- Understand how each scene raises and answers questions for the reader and creates a mini-arc
- Test your scene for scene questions and character changes

MISSING CAUSES AND EFFECTS

For a scene to be clear to the reader, every reaction (the effect) must have a cause. And the cause should come directly before the reaction so it makes sense. Remember our scene with Sunghee and the class election from the last chapter?

"The votes are in, and Sunghee will be our next class president," Miss Mann said.

Sunghee flinched. He raced from the room.

Let's break down the series of causes and effects:

Miss Mann says the votes are in. **[cause]** Sunghee flinches. **[effect]**

??? **[cause]** Sunghee races from the room. **[effect]**

When we look at the scene through the lens of cause and effect, we see that we are missing a cause. Why does Sunghee race from the room? Miss Mann's words don't tell us. And we don't know what Sunghee thinks about her announcement. We are missing a cause for his reaction. The missing cause is Sunghee's thoughts and feelings about winning the election.

What if instead Miss Mann shouted, "Fire!"? Let's break that down into cause and effect:

Miss Mann shouted, "Fire!" **[cause]** Sunghee raced from the room. **[effect]**

In this case, the danger of the situation is clear from Miss Mann's words, and Sunghee reacts just as we expect him to. Internalization isn't necessary.

WHEN CAUSES AND EFFECTS ARE OUT OF ORDER

Missing causes and effects aren't the only issue we can have in a scene. Sometimes writers write causes and effects out of order, which can confuse the reader. For example, what if I had written:

> Sunghee flinched when Miss Mann said, "The votes are in, and Sunghee will be our next class president."

As a reader, I paused for a beat after "Sunghee flinched." I wonder, "Why? What happened?" Momentarily, I am confused because the effect (flinching) came before the cause:

> Sunghee flinched. **[effect]** Miss Mann said the votes are in. **[cause]**

Be kind to your reader. Put the cause before the effect. This version is also problematic:

> "The votes are in, and Sunghee will be our next class president," Miss Mann said.
>
> Sunghee flinched. He raced from the room.
>
> Miss Mann had just assigned a huge class project that would take the whole semester. How would Sunghee have enough time for his presidential duties?

> Miss Mann announced the votes are in. **[cause 1]** Sunghee flinched. **[effect 1]**

??? **[cause 2]** Sunghee raced from the room. **[effect 2]**
Sunghee wondered how he would have time. **[cause 2]**

There is a difference between intriguing your reader by adding a bit of mystery and confusing them. When you confuse your reader, you take them out of the story, giving them an opportunity to put down your book and walk away.

Scene Order: Physical Reaction —> Internalization —> Speech (or Physical Action)

There's a typical order for the scene building blocks used in a character's reaction. When something happens, there is often an instinctive physical response first, like a wince or a grin. Next comes the brief internalization where the character is processing what's just been done or said to them. After they've had a moment to process, the character responds, perhaps with a snippet of speech or by taking the next physical action. This order feels most natural to the reader.

AVOIDING FILTER WORDS AND CREATIVE DIALOGUE TAGS

Let's look at another pair of short paragraphs:

Paragraph 1: The butterflies felt a cool wind blowing in from the north. They saw the sun dipping lower in the sky. It's time to go, they thought.

Paragraph 2: The cold wind blew. The sun dipped lower in the sky. It was time to go.

What do you notice about this paragraph pair (aside from the fact that Paragraph 1 is wordier)?

Paragraph 1 uses **filter words**: "felt," "saw," and "thought." Paragraph 2 does not.

Aside from upping your word count, filter words create narrative distance between the reader and the story. They call attention to themselves, pulling us out of the main character's experience. You don't have to tell me what the character saw, felt, tasted, heard, or thought. I am in the character's head, experiencing what they are experiencing. Just give me the sensory details or the internalization so I can stay in the story.

Similarly, when writing dialogue, use "said" as a dialogue tag as much as you can. "Said" is nearly invisible to the reader. When authors try to get creative with dialogue tags, it can pull the reader out of the story. Here's an example:

"I'm going home!" Jorge snarled.

"You're just being a bad sport!" Helena shouted.

"What are you going to do about it?" Jorge threatened.

The dialogue tags in this excerpt call attention to themselves. Imagine if I had just used "said." Or I could have dropped the dialogue tags altogether and inserted an action, like this:

"I'm going home!" Jorge packed up his soccer ball.

"You're just being a bad sport!" Helena said.

Jorge took a step closer, getting in Helena's face. "What are you going to do about it?"

EXERCISE 10: THE SCENE TEST

Take out the scene you wrote at the end of the last chapter. If you have pens or highlighters in a myriad of colors, now's the time to use them. We are going to analyze your scene for various components.

- First, let's test for cause and effect (action and reaction) in your scene:
- Look at each action.
- What caused it?
- Does the cause come directly before the effect so you're not confusing the reader?
- A good test for this is to write the words "because of that" between every cause and effect. If "because of that" doesn't work, you might have a problem.
- Now test the order of the scene building blocks in your character's reaction. For each reaction, use three different colored pens or highlighters to note physical actions, internalization, and speech. If you don't have colored pens or highlighters, use different marks, like boxing, underlining, and underlining with a squiggle, to indicate the different scene components. Make sure the order for each reaction is right: physical response, internalization, and then speech or another physical action. The last part—the action the character takes—should serve as the cause for the next effect.
- Highlight or circle any filter words and creative dialogue tags in the scene.

When you are finished, make adjustments to your actions and reactions. If you need to, reorder the scene building blocks in your character's response. Then remove any filter words.

———

COMMON FILTER WORDS

- Thought
- Remembered
- Decided
- Realized
- Knew
- Felt
- Saw
- Looked
- Heard
- Tasted
- Smelled

———

SCENES RAISE QUESTIONS

In Chapter 4, which covered narratives, I mentioned that your entire story has a question for the reader: "Will the protagonist achieve their big goal?" That question drives the external plot and keeps your reader turning pages, building tension. Here are some story questions from my books:

- Will Lilian Todd succeed in building her airplane (or will she give up)? (*Wood, Wire, Wings*)
- How did Wonder Woman become the icon she is today? (*A True Wonder*)
- Will Cecilia Payne discover something new just like she's always dreamed? (*The Fire of Stars*)

By pursuing the story question and the plot events that flow from it, your character changes from beginning to end, learning your book's takeaway. If you don't have a main character because your book isn't narrative, it's the reader who learns the takeaway and changes from beginning to end.

But here's something else to consider: scenes are like mini-stories within your larger story. Each scene begins with an implied question. The tension builds as the reader seeks the answer to that question. Then the scene concludes with the answer and implies a new question.

Let's look at the example scenes we've been working with:

From *Wood, Wire, Wings*: "Another day [Lilian] took apart the clock, spreading the pieces before her."

Scene question: Will Lilian get the clock back together?

Reading on: "Did this wheel fit here? Did that lever fit there? She put the pieces back this way. No tick. She put the pieces back that way. No tock. The clock stayed still. Failure! Lilian stood baffled but buoyed by the challenge."

New question: What will Lilian try next?

From our butterfly scene: "A cool wind blows in from the north, and the sun dips lower in the sky. It's time to go."

Scene question: Where will the butterflies go?

Reading on: "The first wing flutters. Then another. A swarm of butterflies flaps, then flies, a whirring blur of orange. Where will they go? Oyamel trees thousands of miles away in Mexico. They must snuggle up before winter arrives."

New question: Will they make it to Mexico in time?

By proposing and answering questions, scenes build anticipation and help move your reader through the story.

SCENES HAVE ARCS

Each scene also contains a mini-narrative arc, creating subtle shifts in our main character or the reader. A main character's mission or their thinking might change through the events of a scene. For Lilian, the clock scene takes her from your average curious kid to someone with a passion for figuring out how machines work. She becomes a person who perseveres despite failure. Yet she still doesn't know what her true life's calling is.

In the butterfly scene, the butterflies begin as carefree, frolicking summertime insects. But by the end of the scene, they are insects on a mission of survival. In both examples, these scenes add to the book's overall arc and takeaway. They are steps on the journey to change.

EXERCISE 11: YOUR SCENE'S QUESTION AND MINI-ARC

Take out the scene you've been working on again and answer the following:

- What is the question raised at the beginning of the scene?
- What is the new question proposed at the end of the scene?
- How would you describe your main character at the beginning of the scene (or, in a non-narrative book, your reader's impression of the subject)?
- How does the character's or your reader's impression change by the end of the scene?

If your scene lacks any of these elements, it's probably falling a bit flat and lacking tension. Go back and revise with an eye toward including scene questions and a mini-arc.

RESEARCH, THE STUFF OF SCENES

Writing scenes is impossible without adequate research. Secondary sources can tell you what happened (plot). But to explain why and how, you need primary sources. Firsthand accounts are critical for crafting internalization and sensory details.

After reading Chapter 10, you will:

- Understand the definitions of primary and secondary sources
- Know why you need each type of source and where to find them
- Understand how to use your research to craft a scene
- Understand the role of research for crafting settings and providing context
- Understand visual research
- Locate sources for your book

RESEARCH CHALLENGES

I was in trouble. I was writing a biography of Lilian Todd, the first woman to design her own airplane, and I didn't have much to go on.

It was bad enough that no one had ever published a biography about her—just a few pages in a biography of her benefactor, Olivia Sage. Even worse, I didn't have much in the way of primary sources: just a few of Lilian's letters, all written after she had stopped building airplanes. No museum had seen fit to save her personal scrapbook. It had sold to a private collector on eBay years before, and he refused to share it. She never wrote an autobiography or kept a diary as far as I could tell.

What could I do?

Newspapers and period magazines saved my story. A woman building an airplane was enough of an oddity in the early 1900s that the newspapers of the time covered Lilian's work constantly. I combed through newspaper databases like the Library of Congress's Chronicling America and a privately maintained database called Old Fulton New York Postcards. I also found an extensive profile of her in *Woman's Home Companion,* a lady's magazine, which included priceless photos.

Through those primary sources, I finally got a glimpse inside Lilian's head and heard her voice. I learned about her childhood, how she became interested in engineering and aviation, and what she hoped to achieve with her airplane. I also learned how she worked: through trial and error, and often starting with models rather than sketches.

Primary sources brought my story to life, and they'll do the same for yours.

WHAT ARE PRIMARY AND SECONDARY SOURCES?

Primary source. You'll find a lot of definitions for the term "primary source" on the internet, but here is one I like from the University of Massachusetts Boston Healey Library. Primary sources are "immediate, firsthand accounts of a topic, from people who had a direct connection with it." These include letters, diaries, newspaper articles, videos (raw footage), photos, and articles from scientific journals that are based on original research, as well as interviews with those researchers.

Secondary source. Meanwhile, the Healey Library defines secondary sources as "one step removed from primary sources, though they often quote or otherwise use primary sources. They can cover the same topic but add a layer of interpretation and analysis." Secondary sources include most books (including biographies), documentaries, and articles by historians, for example.

WHY YOU NEED SECONDARY SOURCES

You need both primary and secondary sources for your nonfiction picture book. Secondary sources provide needed context. They show how your specific subject fits into the historical or scientific landscape. Nobody operates in a vacuum.

For example, it's not enough to know that Lilian Todd was building an airplane; I needed to know why her work mattered. That meant understanding the aviation landscape of the time, including the roles of major players like the Wright brothers, Alberto Santos-Dumont, and Glenn Curtiss. I also had to understand the role of smaller builders who were competing for cash prizes that pushed airplanes higher, faster, and farther. I found this information in books and historical articles—secondary sources.

The other benefit of secondary sources is that good ones contain detailed bibliographies. That means secondary sources can lead you to primary sources like newspaper articles, letters and papers, or research studies.

For example, I didn't know about Lilian Todd's few scattered letters located at Auburn University until I read the biography of her benefactor, Olivia Sage. I didn't know where the papers of Wonder Woman's creator, William Moulton Marston, were housed until after I read *The Secret History of Wonder Woman* by Jill Lepore and found them at Harvard. That book also pointed me to the papers of psychiatrist Dr. Lauretta Bender, which were located at Brooklyn College and gave me insight into how the comic was revised during the editing process. I was able to visit and research both collections.

WHY YOU NEED PRIMARY SOURCES

Writing a biography is a lot like acting. You must get into character. Primary sources help you do that by providing motivation and personality. They help you get inside your subject's head. Primary sources also give you their voice in the form of quotes you can incorporate into your scenes. No matter what you are writing, primary sources provide sensory details like sounds, smells, and visual descriptions from people who were there. It's hard to get those details anywhere else.

Yet primary sources aren't just for biographies, histories, and other narratives. They also are critical for expository writing about the natural world. Remember the paragraph I made up about butterflies in Chapter 8? To know what a flapping mass of butterflies looked and sounded like, I watched a video of monarch butterfly migration. Only then could I accurately describe the colors of the butterflies and the "whirring" sound they made. If I hadn't been able to find a video, I might have interviewed a butterfly researcher who studied butterflies in the field and could describe the experience of being there.

Finally, what we know about science and history changes every day. Secondary sources can quickly become dated. The most accurate information comes from people working in the field, who are researching and publishing their findings right now.

FROM PRIMARY SOURCE TO SCENE

How do you get from primary sources to a scene? Most of the time, you need to combine pieces of research from different sources to bring your scene to life.

Here are a couple of snippets I used to build the clock scene in *Wood, Wire, Wings*. The first is from *Woman's Home Companion* (1909).

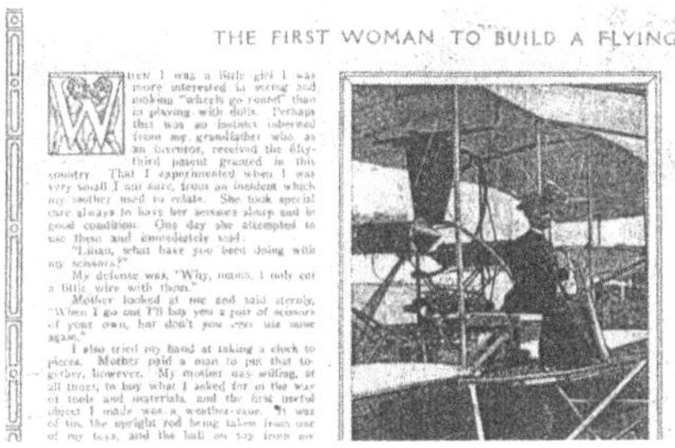

This article gave me several pieces of information for the clock scene:

- Lilian's tinkering nature, using anything available to her
- Evidence that she took the clock apart and tried to put it together again
- Evidence that she failed

By itself, the *Woman's Home Companion* article wasn't enough to build the scene. I also needed to understand Lilian's relationship to failure. Why didn't she give up or get frustrated? Here is another article from the *New-York Tribune* (November 20, 1910) that speaks to the subject:

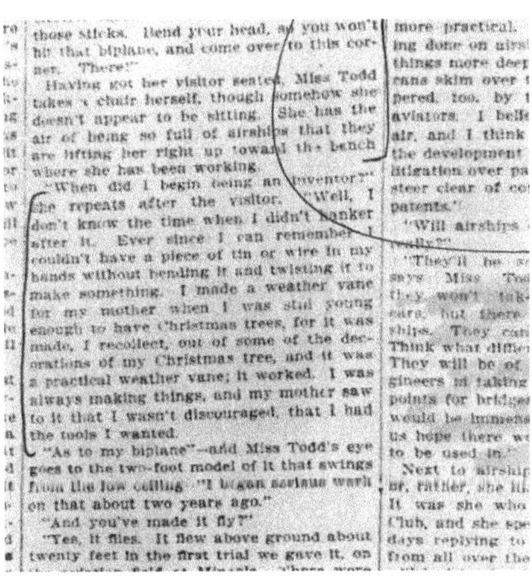

This gave me:

- More evidence about how Lilian worked (tinkering)
- The quote that appears on the two-page spread with the clock scene: "I was always making things, and my mother saw to it that I wasn't discouraged, that I had the tools I wanted."
- Evidence of Lilian's nature—she didn't get discouraged by failure. Her mother wouldn't let her.

Did I have everything I needed to write the scene? Almost.

RESEARCH INTO SETTING AND TIME PERIOD

What did a household clock in the 1860s look like? I couldn't describe the process of taking one apart and putting it back together if I didn't know what a typical 1860s clock looked like in America. And how would I know what it sounded like? Did it even make a tick-tock sound? Chasing down the specifics of an 1860s mantle clock required a lot of research and was surprisingly difficult.

This type of indirect research is often necessary to bring sensory details to your scene. You can't write a scene about Amazonian poison dart frogs without understanding the Amazon. You must learn all you can about rainforests and the animals that live there, including the sounds, smells, sights, and physical sensations you might encounter.

PUTTING IT ALL TOGETHER

How long did tracking down this information take? A long time. Research is painstaking. Still, from the sources mentioned above (among others), I could write this 53-word scene:

Another day [Lilian] took apart the clock, spreading the pieces before her. Did this wheel fit here? Did that lever fit there? She put the pieces back this way. No tick. She put the pieces back that way. No tock. The clock stayed still. Failure! Lilian stood baffled but buoyed by the challenge.

Research proved much easier with *The Fire of Stars* since Cecilia Payne-Gaposchkin had written an autobiography and given an oral history. I found details for the scenes from Cecilia's childhood in those primary sources. I did need to do some indirect research into bee orchids and the landscape of Buckinghamshire, England, where Cecilia grew up. Still, finding an autobiography, diary, or letters makes the research go far more quickly!

If I were thoroughly researching for my butterfly scene example, I would have needed multiple sources of research, too. I might have hunted down a journal article from a butterfly scientist to understand their migration cues. If that had left me with unanswered questions, I would have contacted the scientist directly. To get the sensory details needed for the scene, I could have either observed them myself on a research trip or watched a documentary showing how they migrate, how their flapping wings sound, and so on. Again, writing a scene like this requires combining research from a variety of sources.

A NOTE ON ACCURACY

One note about firsthand accounts: make sure you corroborate as much as you can, especially dates and other facts. Human memory is notoriously faulty when it comes to names, dates, places, and other specific details. Autobiographies and even letters written a few days after the fact often get things wrong. Validate information from your research by comparing it to other sources, including secondary sources pulled together by experts who study the time you are writing about. I rely on biographies and memoirs more for emotional truths and sensory details.

No matter what you are writing, always consider your source. In autobiographies and memoirs, the writer often casts themself in the most favorable light. Scientific and historical sources can have their biases, too, especially if the authors are writing outside their own cultural background or decades ago.

Today, we know the Earth orbits the Sun. Prior to the discoveries of Galileo in the 1600s, people thought the Sun orbited the Earth. That fit neatly with much of Western Europe's religious views. If I relied on research from the 1500s, I might inaccurately write that the Sun orbits the Earth.

It's also important to know if your scientific source is an outlier. Even if the majority of scientific or historical evidence points to one conclusion, there will always be studies showing the opposite. Have other researchers replicated or validated your source's findings? You can find out what other scientists or historians think of your source's work by reading reviews of research, which often appear in journals.

VISUAL RESEARCH FOR THE ILLUSTRATOR

Nonfiction illustrators have different appetites for research. With that in mind, your editor or illustrator may ask you to share your sources containing visual details. For *Wood, Wire, Wings*, editor Carolyn Yoder asked me to provide an art reference file for illustrator Tracy Subisak, including images and visual descriptions. Pieces like the *Woman's Home Companion* article, which showed what Lilian and her airplane looked like in 1909, were a gold mine.

The Fire of Stars illustrator, Katherine Roy, writes and illustrates her own books, and she loves research. She did her own visual research for *The Fire of Stars* and only asked me to double-check one detail: what Cecilia Payne's college completion certificate looked like since women weren't granted degrees at the time. That was not easy to find!

Even if you aren't providing visual research sources to the illustrator, you must know what items from your chosen time period look like so you can check the illustrations for accuracy. Nonfiction authors usually review illustration sketches, called dummies, for accuracy before the illustrator moves to finished artwork.

Despite painstaking research, nearly every book has something that's not quite right in the dummy illustrations. In *A True Wonder*, Katy Wu originally drew a scene between Bill Marston and tennis pro

Alice Marble against a backdrop of palm trees. My text didn't explain that the scene occurred in New York. We had to take out the palm trees.

In *Wood, Wire, Wings*, Tracy Subisak initially drew the clock Lilian took apart as a 1950s-style alarm clock with two bells. Those didn't exist until much later.

When you are conducting your primary source research, pay careful attention to visual research sources, including detailed descriptions, and keep them in a special spot so you can share them with your illustrator if requested. You do not need to share all these details in lengthy illustrators' notes. Let the illustrator (or the editor as the middleperson) ask for what they need or discover it on their own.

YOUR TURN

Go back to the scene you've been working on and ask yourself what it's missing. Do you need to hunt down your character's motivation? A sensory detail? Where might you find what you need?

Keep track of the evidence you use for each scene. I often footnote as I go, so I know exactly where I pulled each bit of information. It's difficult to cite and organize your research after the fact. I write in Scrivener, which makes footnoting simple, but you can footnote in Microsoft Word, too.

THE SCENE-LEVEL REWRITE

It's time for the second of our three major rewrites, the scene-level rewrite. I hope you are as excited as I am!

Take out your work in progress and do the following:

- What parts of your story need to be written as scenes for maximum tension and emotion? Look back at Chapter 8, where I discussed some key moments you might want to write in scene.
- What parts of your story can you summarize?

- For the portions you've identified that must be in scene, rewrite your book one scene at a time.
- For each scene, first let the scene play out in your mind like a mini-movie and imagine the voiceover narration.
- Write the text for that voiceover. That's your scene.
- Now evaluate. Use colored pens, highlighters, or boxes/squiggles/underlines to indicate physical actions, internalization, speech, sensory details, and vivid verbs.
- See if you can insert "because of that" between each cause and effect. Does every action or choice have a cause, which produces an effect and leads to the next action?
- Are your causes and effects in the proper order so you don't confuse your reader?
- If causes and effects don't make sense, do you need to add internalization? Remember the proper order: physical reaction internalization speech (or physical action).
- Does each scene begin with an implied question? Is that question answered through the scene, logically leading to a new question?
- Is your scene a mini-arc that produces a small change in your main character or the reader? Does it add to the overall arc of the story?
- Highlight and then remove any filter words and creative dialogue tags.
- Take the time to locate the research sources you need for authentic motivation, dialogue, and sensory details. Footnote where you found those details so you don't have to do it later.

Congratulations! You've completed the second of our three major revisions. You've finished the hard part. Our final rewrite, the voice rewrite, will be nowhere near as time consuming. That's what we're moving on to now.

SECTION 4: VIBRANT VOICE

CHAPTER 11
USING VOICE TO MAKE MUSIC

Picture books are meant to be read aloud by an adult to a child. That means your words must make music and paint pictures in the minds of your readers.

After you read Chapter 11, you will:

- Understand what voice is
- Know the aspects of voice that make picture books musical
- Add musicality to your work in progress

NOT A RESEARCH PAPER

Rewind to a full year before I had the idea to add a parallel storyline to *The Fire of Stars*. The manuscript was falling flat, and I couldn't figure out why. Here's a sample from the early draft:

Revision 1

Young Cecilia spent hours outside watching slimy slugs slink through her garden, picking out constellations in the night sky, and counting trees among her best friends.

She planned to be a botanist, a plant scientist. She would research and discover new things all on her own. Her greatest fear was that everything would be figured out by the time she grew up. Lucky for Cecilia, she lived in a time when science changed everything.

When she turned 12, Cecilia's family moved from the country, and she said good-bye to her precious trees and hello to the smokestacks of London. [100 words]

It's not horrible. I have some nice sensory details and vivid verbs in there, like the slimy slugs slinking. But somehow, the passage just doesn't sing.

When I wrote this draft, I still thought of writing nonfiction picture books as akin to writing a college research paper. That meant writing complete sentences with subjects and predicates, or long sentences with lots of clauses. And it meant using lots of boring periods instead of more interesting punctuation.

What shifted my thinking? In summer 2016, I took Renée LaTulippe's "Lyrical Language Lab" class, which I recommend to any writer, whether or not you aspire to be a poet. Renée's class helped me look at nonfiction picture books as poetry, even when they don't rhyme.

Poems focus on a moment in time. They use sensory detail and clever analogies to bring scenes to life. They make music. *That's* what I wanted, not a Ph.D. thesis (though I felt like I'd done enough research on Cecilia Payne that I could write one!). Taking the ideas from Renée's class to heart, I started working on a revision to the above passage during that very class. Here is the result:

Revision 2

Cecilia spends hours
watching slimy slugs glide through the garden
and making friends with trees and flowers …
Cecilia realizes all by herself why an orchid has a petal like a bee's belly.

To trick the bees, of course!

They buzz over to say hello to their pretend friend,

then fly off with pollen-stuffed pockets—the start of new seeds.

Cecilia buzzes, too—her body humming with that lightning bolt of discovery.

She wants to feel that way forever.

Yet the fields and flowers, so full of inspiration for Cecilia, are not enough for her family.

Soon everything shifts and separates—

Mother trades the soil and starry country skies

for the sooty smokestacks of London

where Cecilia's brother Humfry can attend a better school.

Cecilia is forced to say hello to city streets full of strangers and

good-bye to the company of trees and bees. [144 words]

Look at Revisions 1 and 2 carefully. What do you notice? What differences do you detect between the two? What kinds of words did I choose? What about my punctuation and so on?

Here are some things you may have noticed:

- Revision 2 is longer.
- Revision 2 adds a little scene with Cecilia's discovery of the flower that looks like a bee.
- Revision 2 is in the present tense, while Revision 1 is in the past tense.
- Revision 1 uses complete sentences, while Revision 2 uses fragments.
- Revision 2 uses more interesting punctuation like **em dashes** and **ellipses**.
- Revision 2 is more fun to read aloud.

With Revision 2, I shifted to a **lyrical voice** that infused my story with a sense of wonder, discovery, and a lot more emotional resonance.

That is the power of voice. Along with developing a strong takeaway and writing in scenes, using vibrant voice is one of the most powerful tools for eliciting emotion in our books and readers. (Illustration style plays a role, too, but unless you are an author-illustrator, you probably won't get a choice in art direction.)

Crafting voice isn't magic. It starts with understanding what voice is, the different components that contribute to voice, and how to use them.

Like story structure, your voice should match your subject and takeaway. A lyrical voice is appropriate for a picture book where I wanted young readers to fall in love with the quest for discovery. A humorous voice wouldn't fit my takeaway and topic, but it's perfect for a book about the history of underwear (see Hannah Holt's *A History of Underwear with Professor Chicken*, illustrated by Korwin Briggs).

WHAT IS VOICE?

Ask one hundred writers what voice is, and you'll get one hundred answers. Here is a definition I like from The Book Designer: "… '[V]oice' refers to the mixture of tone, word choice, point of view, syntax, punctuation, and rhythm that make up sentences and paragraphs."

Newbery author Linda Sue Park states it a bit more simply:

voice = word choice + rhythm
    rhythm = sentence length + punctuation

For the purposes of this book, we'll start with Linda Sue Park's definition. However, we'll also consider the role of point of view, which is included in The Book Designer's definition.

EXERCISE 12: DISSECTING VOICE

Before I discuss the components of voice, let's analyze a passage from a nonfiction picture book. Grab a favorite off your shelf, preferably one that matches the voice you are going for in your current draft. Consider:

- What do you notice about the voice components (word choice, sentence length, punctuation)?
- How would you characterize this voice? Is it lyrical, humorous, active, playful?
- How does it make you feel?
- How well does the voice match the subject matter and the takeaway?
- What elements contribute to this book's voice?

OUR VOICE TOOLBOX: SOUND DEVICES

A big part of a picture book's read-aloud factor and a reader's emotional response comes from word choice, specifically our use of sound devices. Sound devices give writing musicality. First let's define the different sound devices we have available to us, and then we'll see how we can use them.

- **Alliteration:** When words that are close together start with the same letter or sound, like "**s**limy **s**lugs **s**link" from Revision 2. The "s" sound is repeated in three words, which is alliteration.
- **Assonance:** When words that are close together have the same vowel sound, like "p**o**llen-stuffed p**o**ckets" from Revision 2. "Pollen" and "pockets" both have the short "o" sound. That's assonance.
- **Consonance:** When words close to each other have the same consonant sound anywhere in the words. In Revision 2, I wrote the following sentence: "Her **g**reatest fear was that everything would be figured out by the time she **g**rew up."

In that sentence, the hard "g" sound is repeated multiple times in "**g**reatest," "fi**g**ured," and "**g**rew." In consonance, the repeated sound isn't always at the beginning of the word; otherwise it would be alliteration.

- **Internal rhyme:** Words that rhyme have the same ending sound. If we write in rhyme, we're establishing a set pattern of rhyming words at the end of each line. If we aren't writing in full rhyme, we can still use internal rhyme, which is when words within a line or sentence rhyme. For example, in Revision 2, I wrote, "They buzz over to say hello to their **pretend friend**." "Pretend" and "friend" rhyme.

- **Repetition:** When a word or a phrase is repeated. I don't have a good example in my samples from above, but if you read Kevin Noble Maillard's *Fry Bread*, you'll see a great example of repetition. Nearly every spread starts with the repeated phrase "Fry bread is …"

- **Onomatopoeia:** When a word imitates the sound we hear. Think of those classic superhero fight words—"BAM," "POW," and "BANG!"—which I used in my Wonder Woman book, *A True Wonder*. In Revision 2 above, I said the bees buzzed over. "Buzz" is a bit of onomatopoeia, since the word imitates the sound a bee makes.

PRACTICAL TIPS FOR SENTENCE TRANSFORMATIONS

I rely on two major tools time and time again to add music to my writing: Thesaurus.com and Rhymezone.com. Thesaurus.com is an online thesaurus that provides synonyms for any word. Rhymezone is a rhyming dictionary. Even though I don't write in rhyme, this site is very helpful for crafting internal rhyme and assonance. Here's how I use the tools for sentence transformations:

1. Let's begin with the sentence "The kite flies through the air."

2. I plug the word "fly" into Rhymezone and see that "sky" rhymes with fly. That's a synonym for air. So one option might be, "The kite flies through the sky." [internal rhyme]
3. But "fly" isn't the most exciting verb. What else could I use? I open Thesaurus.com and look for synonyms for "fly." Here are some that jumped out at me: "float," "flutter," "glide," "sail," "swoop," "soar." I could try:

"The kite glides through the sky." [assonance]
  "The kite swoops through the sky." [alliteration]
  "The kite soars through the sky." [alliteration]

Each option contributes to the voice in a different way. If I were writing with a more humorous or active voice, I might pick "swoop." Otherwise, if I were writing in a lyrical voice, I might choose "The kite glides through the sky."

Using Thesaurus.com and Rhymezone.com, you can brainstorm a list of words to try out—a word bank.

EXERCISE 13: MAKING MUSIC

Go back to one of your picture book mentor texts and type out a particularly striking paragraph or scene of approximately 100 words. Now comes the fun part. See what sound devices you can find. Use different colored pens, highlighters, or marks to mark up the different sound devices we've discussed. How do these sound devices add to the effects? What feeling do they create?

Just for fun, take a few lines from your work in progress and apply sound devices in a similar way. Use Thesaurus.com and Rhymezone.com to craft a word bank first. Then explore your options, trying out different combinations.

CHAPTER 12
FEEL THE RHYTHM

f you're a musician, you know that rhythm gives music its heartbeat, determining how fast or slow the piece moves. In this way, rhythm contributes to the pace and emotion of the piece.

In nonfiction picture books, we don't have a drum kit, but we do have other tools to create rhythmic effects. These include word choice and length, sentence length, and punctuation.

After reading Chapter 12, you will:

- Hear the differences between various rhythms
- Understand the tools used to achieve rhythmic effects, including word and punctuation choices
- Add rhythm to your work in progress

RHYTHMIC EFFECTS: LONG AND SHORT

Let's start by listening to a couple of pieces of music.

First imagine a swooping, soaring symphony. I'm a big fan of Beethoven's *Symphony No. 3* if you need a suggestion; you can find it on a music app or YouTube. Notice how the notes are held for longer and seem to blend into each other, an effect called **legato**, meaning long.

Now contrast that with Dave Brubeck's jazz classic "Take Five," which is active and lively. The notes are clipped nd distinct, and the playing style is more **staccato**, meaning short.

In music, these long and short effects are created by holding the notes for a long or short time and using (or not using) rests or pauses between notes. In writing, we have other tools we can use to create these long and short effects. Let's explore these tools using a couple of passages from my books as a reference point.

> **Passage 1 from** *The Fire of Stars*
> Soon everything shifts
> and separates—
> Mother trades the soil and starry country skies
> for the sooty smokestacks of London,
> where Cecilia's brother Humfry can attend
> a better school.

> **Passage 2 from** *Wood, Wire, Wings*
> Another day [Lilian] took apart the clock, spreading the pieces before her. Did this wheel fit here? Did that lever fit there? She put the pieces back this way. No tick. She put the pieces back that way. No tock. The clock stayed still. Failure! Lilian stood baffled but buoyed by the challenge.

In your notebook, reflect:

- How would you describe the voice of these two passages?
- How would you describe their rhythm? Is one more like Beethoven and the other more like Brubeck (long versus short)?

- Now look closer. What do you notice about the punctuation I used?
- What do you notice about my word choices and the sounds they make? Think back to the sound devices we covered in the last chapter and how they are working in these passages.

THE ROLE OF PUNCTUATION AND SENTENCE LENGTH IN CREATING RHYTHM

Think of punctuation as the rests in a piece of music. Periods, commas, em dashes, ellipses, and other punctuation marks separate or connect ideas and tell us whether to pause, stop, or keep reading.

For example, I would characterize Passage 1 from *The Fire of Stars* as legato, smoother and more flowing like the Beethoven symphony. If you read the whole book, you'll notice the length of the sentences. They often are quite long, requiring commas to separate the ideas. Commas are a softer form of punctuation than periods and can add to the legato effect. I also use em dashes and ellipses, which help connect the ideas and weave a sense of wonder. The pace is slower. That's the legato effect, which contributes to the lyrical voice.

Contrast that excerpt with *Wood, Wire, Wings* in Passage 2. The sentences in this example are shorter. Some are even fragments. I don't use commas, em dashes, or ellipses. Instead, I bring sentences to a full stop with periods and emphasize the word "failure" with an exclamation point. This passage is more staccato, with a quicker pace that resembles Brubeck's composition. The punctuation I've chosen adds to that active, lively voice.

To summarize, here's how punctuation influences voice:

- Legato rhythm with slower pacing and a more lyrical, wondrous voice often relies on:
- Longer sentences or lines
- Commas or semicolons separating clauses
- Em dashes (—) or ellipses (…) to connect ideas and blend one into another

- Staccato rhythm with quicker pacing and more lively and active voice often relies on:
- Shorter sentences
- Periods
- Exclamation points (used sparingly)

THE ROLE OF WORD CHOICE IN RHYTHM

Remember from the last chapter that word choice can add musicality to our writing when we use sound devices. At the same time, our word choices can create different sound effects, whether soft or hard, long or short.

Look again at Passages 1 and 2, and listen to the sounds the words make. What consonant sounds do you hear? What about vowel sounds?

In Passage 1 and throughout *The Fire of Stars*, I use a lot of soft sounds, like "s" (or the soft "c" of "Cecilia") and "sh." Long vowel sounds, like in "trade" and "sky," add to this soft or legato effect. And this in turn adds to the lyrical, wonder-filled voice.

In Passage 2 from *Wood, Wire, Wings*, I use a lot of harder sounds, like the hard "k" sound in "clock," "tick," and "tock." The "b" sounds in "baffled yet buoyed" are also shorter and harder. Plus, I use vowel sounds in words like "tick" and "tock." All these word choices contribute to the staccato effect.

To summarize, here's how word choice influences voice:

- Long (legato) rhythm with slower pacing and a more lyrical, wondrous voice often relies on:
- Softer consonant sounds
- Long vowel sounds
- Short (staccato) rhythm with quicker pacing and more lively and active voice often relies on:
- Harder consonant sounds
- Short vowel sounds

EXERCISE 14: ANALYZING RHYTHM

Grab any picture book off your shelf, preferably nonfiction. Type out a particularly good section of about 100 words. How would you characterize the voice? Now analyze the rhythm. You might use different colored pens, highlighters, or marks to highlight punctation, vowel sounds, and consonant sounds.

- What do you notice about the punctuation? Is it hard (exclamation points, periods) or soft (commas, ellipses, em dashes)?
- Are sentences or lines long or short?
- Are the vowel sounds long or short?
- Are the consonant sounds hard or soft?
- How do these sounds contribute to the rhythm and the voice?

RHYTHM IS A CONTINUUM

You can typically describe the overall voice of a book with a single word: humorous, wondrous, peaceful, soothing, and so on. And each type of voice tends toward a certain rhythm. Humorous, active, lively, playful voices tend to have a more staccato rhythm. Wondrous, lyrical, soothing voices tend to have a more legato rhythm.

But books are not necessarily wholly legato or staccato. Rhythm exists on a continuum. Often writers play with rhythm to control the way the reader experiences the book. A writer may use shorter sentences, harder punctuation and consonants, and short vowel sounds to pick up the pace in a particular scene and encourage the reader to read faster. When an author wants you to slow down and pay attention, they may infuse a scene with more legato techniques like softer consonants, long vowel sounds, and softer punctuation.

And sometimes they might insert a wordless spread—a full rest—for emphasis. Once you've mastered rhythm tools, you can play with them in this way.

TIPS FOR GETTING INTO VOICE

Getting into voice has a lot in common with an actor getting into character. It takes effort. Two of the best ways I know of getting into voice are to:

1. Read aloud a lot of books that use the voice you want to emulate to get a feel for the rhythm and musicality.
2. Type out passages from those same books. This transcription process forces you to slow down and study what makes the passages work. Then you can apply those same techniques to your own work.

CHAPTER 13
PAINTING PICTURES

Vibrant voice doesn't just sound musical; it also paints pictures in the minds of your readers.

After reading Chapter 13, you will:

- Understand the major components of **figurative** language
- Know how vivid verbs and sensory details add to voice
- Incorporate these new elements into your existing work in progress

FIGURATIVE LANGUAGE: AN EXAMPLE

I made some changes to the butterfly passage we used in our previous chapters. Let's read the original passage and the revised version, and then we'll analyze them:

Passage 1: A cool wind blows in from the north, and the sun dips lower in the sky. It's time to go. The first wing flutters. Then another. A swarm of butterflies flaps, then flies, a whirring blur of orange. Where will they go? Oyamel trees thousands of miles away in Mexico. They must snuggle up before winter arrives.

Passage 2: The wind blows, cold as snow, from the north. The sun dips lower in the sky. The butterflies know it's time to go. The first wing flutters. Then another. A swarm of butterflies flaps, then flies, a whirring symphony of orange. Where will they go? Oyamel trees a lifetime away in Mexico. They must snuggle up before winter arrives.

Compare and contrast the two paragraphs. How do they make you feel? What sort of mental pictures do they create? What words or phrases conjure those mental pictures?

VOICE TOOLS: FIGURATIVE LANGUAGE PAINTS MENTAL PICTURES

Merriam-Webster has the simplest definition of figurative language: "words or phrases that are meaningful, but not literally true." Figurative language can exaggerate or draw comparisons to create surprising connections, evoke emotion, or aid a young reader's understanding by connecting a new idea with something that's already familiar.

Here are the main figurative tools:

Metaphor is the nonliteral comparison between objects or actions. From Passage 2, the phrase "whirring symphony of orange" uses a metaphor to compare the butterflies with a symphony orchestra. Are the butterflies really an orchestra with tiny instruments? Not literally. Yet the metaphor emphasizes the idea of the sound (whirring) and the idea that the butterflies are moving together as one.

Simile is a comparison typically using "like" or "as." From Passage 2, I used the simile "cold as snow." Is the wind literally snowy? Nope. But I wanted the reader to understand just how cold the wind was. That's a better choice than stating an exact temperature, since many kids are familiar with snow and how cold it feels.

Personification is when you give a nonhuman item human characteristics. In Passages 1 and 2, I wrote, "They must snuggle up before winter arrives." Snuggling suggests a bit of personification. In Passage 2, I added, "The butterflies know it's time to go." Are the butterflies sentient beings with higher-order cognitive processing like a person? No. But I wanted to convey how the wind and the lowering sun were sending a signal to the butterflies and what the butterflies' response was.

Hyperbole is dramatic overstatement. In Passage 2, I wrote the oyamel trees are "a lifetime away." It's only a bit of an overstatement, because the butterflies that fly to Mexico will never return home. Instead, they will lay eggs, and those offspring will begin the journey back north.

What effect does this bit of hyperbole produce? Well, in Passage 1, I wrote that the butterflies' journey is a thousand miles. A child may not have the context to understand just how far that is. Plus, kids may make regular trips of thousands of miles to see relatives far away via car or airplane. To them, it may not seem like such a big deal. Adding the hyperbole "a lifetime away" shows just how big this journey is in the context of a butterfly's life, aiding the reader's understanding.

Understatement is making a situation seem less than it is. I don't have a good example in either of my passages, but my all-time favorite is from the movie *Monty Python and the Holy Grail*. In the film the Knights of the Round Table encounter a black knight who won't let them pass. King Arthur fights the knight, cuts off his arm, and demands that he concede. The knight responds, "'Tis nothing but a scratch!" as blood spurts from his wound. Clearly the wound is more severe than a scratch. That's understatement. Often understatement is used for humor.

Figurative language can aid a reader's understanding of the information they're reading, while also adding beauty, surprise, and emotion to your writing.

VOICE TOOLS: SENSORY DETAILS AND VIVID VERBS

We discussed the need for sensory details and vivid verbs in Section 3, "Scene Writing." I want to reemphasize them here because the vivid verbs and sensory details you choose add to the voice of your manuscript.

For example, the verbs "skitter," "scoot," and "ricochet" all mean something similar but create completely different pictures. "Ricochet" could be wonderful in a manuscript with a humorous voice. "Skitter" might work well in a manuscript with a more lyrical voice, especially if you could use it as a starting point for incorporating sound devices. For example, if you choose "skitter," you might use "glitter," "patter," or "simmer" nearby to create internal rhyme or assonance.

EXERCISE 15: USE BREVETTES TO PRACTICE WITH VIVID VERBS

I learned about the brevette, a poetry form created by Emily Romano, in Georgia Heard's and Rebecca Kai Dotlich's "The Poet's Studio" workshop. These brief poems are a wonderful way to limber up before you write because they force you to consider vivid verbs.

A brevette is a three-line poem. There is only one word per line. Here is the pattern:

subject (noun)

verb

object (noun)

The idea is to strive for nonliteral and surprising noun/verb combinations. Use your imagination and be playful. Here's a brevette I wrote:

Buds

W h i s p e r

Spring

Note the bit of personification with "whisper" since flower buds don't really whisper.

Writing in any poetic form, including simple, nonrhyming forms like haiku, spine poetry, or list poems, can help you unlock figurative language and get into voice. There is a poetry form index at The Poet's Collective that I hope will inspire you.

EXERCISE 16: WORD LADDERS

This exercise comes from Wilco front man, Jeff Tweedy, and his book *How to Write One Song*, which I highly recommend. Songwriting and writing poetic, voice-rich prose have much in common.

- Turn to a blank sheet of paper in your writer's notebook and draw a line down the center of the page. Title the left column "Verbs" and the right column "Nouns."
- In the left column, write down ten verbs associated with an airline pilot, a baker, or any other profession.
- In the right column, write down ten objects you can see in your room.
- Draw lines between nouns and verbs, striving for pairs that normally wouldn't make sense together or that are surprising.
- Then write a couple of lines of poetry or a whole poem using some of your word pairs.

EXERCISE 17: RAISE YOUR VOICE

There's nothing more fun than trying to add verve to an encyclopedia entry. For the passage below, choose a voice (humorous, lyrical, active, playful, etc.) and rewrite a portion of the passage, considering rhythm, sound devices, and figurative language. Don't be afraid to unleash your creativity!

Seahorses are rather immobile, swimming more slowly than other fishes. When swimming they maintain a vertical position and propel themselves forward using a soft-rayed dorsal fin. They use pectoral fins located on the side of the head to maneuver. Some scientists contend that this upright swimming posture evolved shortly after the expansion of sea grasses in the western Pacific roughly 25 million years ago. These plants provided seahorses with useful hiding places to avoid enemies and to capture unsuspecting prey, and ancestors of the seahorse evolved to maximize the opportunities offered by this new habitat.

Seahorses are usually found clinging to plants or corals with their tails. Their sedentary habits coupled with excellent camouflage abilities render them successful ambush predators. When small organisms swim nearby, a seahorse may capture them by rapidly sucking them into the mouth. Seahorses also rely upon camouflage to avoid predators such as crabs and other fishes. (from *Encyclopedia Britannica*)

How did you do? Did you achieve your intended voice? What do you think added to the effects?

Once you are finished, go back to your work in progress and analyze:

- How would you characterize the voice of your manuscript?
- Is it appropriate for your subject matter and takeaway?
- Revise one spread of your work in progress (approximately 100 words) using the techniques we discussed to enhance your voice, including sound devices, figurative language, sensory details, and rhythm.

Don't revise the whole thing yet, though. We still have a few more matters to discuss.

POINT OF VIEW AND VERB TENSE

Switching up your point of view (POV), perspective, or verb tense can add to voice and alter the mood of your manuscript. After reading Chapter 14, you will:

- Understand three major points of view, how to recognize them, and how to use them
- Understand perspective
- Understand the three major tenses
- Know how POV and tense contribute to voice

THREE POINTS OF VIEW

You probably learned about POV years ago in school, but it may have been a while. Don't worry! We're going to review it now. Here are the major points of view:

- First person (I)
- Second person (you/we)
- Third person (he/she/it/they)

THIRD PERSON (HE/SHE/IT/THEY)

We're starting with third person because it is the most common POV for nonfiction picture books. If I had to guess, I'd say 90 percent of nonfiction picture books are in third person, including almost all picture book biographies. Here's an example from *The Fire of Stars*, which you've seen before:

Passage 1

Cecilia realizes all by herself why an orchid has a petal like a bee's belly.

To trick the bees, of course!

They buzz over to say hello to their pretend friend,

then fly off with pollen-stuffed pockets—the start of new seeds.

Cecilia buzzes, too—her body humming with that lightning bolt of discovery.

She wants to feel that way forever.

Yet the fields and flowers, so full of inspiration for Cecilia, are not enough for her family.

Soon everything shifts and separates—

The big tip-off that you are dealing with third person is the use of the character's name, for example "Cecilia realizes" or the pronouns "he," "she," "it," or "they."

One advantage of third-person POV is its flexibility. It can be used to craft almost any voice from humorous to wondrous. Children are very familiar with third person, since it's used in most fiction picture books as well.

One potential downside of third-person POV is that it can create some distance between your story and the reader, rather than allowing them to insert themselves into the story. One work-around is to use close third person, in which the reader experiences the thoughts and emotions of the main character. When you learned how to craft scenes using minute-by-minute action and internalization, you were learning how to write in close third person. You can write in more objective third person, but this creates more narrative distance.

FIRST PERSON (I/WE)

First-person POV is not commonly used in nonfiction picture books, so it can be surprising and refreshing when readers encounter it. One reason it's not used is because first person can transform our books from strict nonfiction into informational fiction. In informational fiction, the primary purpose of the picture book is to inform, but elements of the book are made up. Sometimes the narrator is fictional; other times plot elements are made up, too.

No matter how well-researched your book, narrating from first person makes your biography fiction, because you are not the person you are writing about. Meanwhile, autobiographies or memoirs are almost always in first person because they are firsthand accounts. These are nonfiction.

Sometimes books get a bit tricky to categorize. In Henry Herz's wonderful book *I Am Smoke*, illustrated by Mercè López, smoke narrates the story, telling readers riddles about itself that add to its mysterious nature. *I Am Smoke* features personification, or giving human emotion and powers of communication to an inanimate object. This makes the book informational fiction. Smoke can't think or feel.

Likewise, in *Over and Under the Waves* by Kate Messner, illustrated by Christopher Silas Neal, Messner creates a fictitious child narrator who explores the hidden world of the kelp forest under the waves during a kayaking trip. The story is narrated in first person, with the character sharing her experiences, talking to her mom, and sharing her sense of wonder at all she discovers. The narrator is not a real person; this makes the book informational fiction.

In *We Are Still Here!* by Traci Sorell, illustrated by Frané Lessac, Sorell uses the collective first person—"we"—to narrate the story of the Native American Nation. Since Sorell is a member of the Cherokee nation, "we" is accurate, and she can use this POV without pushing the book into informational fiction.

Why would an author adopt a perspective that might fictionalize their story? First-person POV is as close as you can get to the character. It puts your reader into the main character's head, filtering everything through their eyes and experience. That closeness can evoke strong emotions in your reader, perhaps awe, wonder, or even humor when an animal or inanimate object talks about itself.

AN ASIDE ABOUT INFORMATIONAL FICTION

There is nothing inherently good or bad about transforming your book from nonfiction into informational fiction. You must do what is best for your manuscript. If you want a child to read a book from start to finish, you must tell the story in the most interesting way possible. Sometimes that means fictionalizing elements of the story. That's okay. The American Library Association's Robert F. Sibert Informational Book Medal, one of the highest awards for informational books, isn't for nonfiction. Instead, it's "awarded annually to the author(s) and illustrator(s) of the most distinguished informational book published in the United States in English during the preceding year." Informational books include books technically classified as informational fiction.

If you write informational fiction, I encourage you to play fair with your reader (and your agent and your editor) by telling them what parts of the manuscript you made up and classifying your book properly as informational fiction. Still, you ultimately can't control how your publisher markets your book or where librarians shelve it. Publishers sometimes market informational fiction books as nonfiction.

SECOND PERSON (YOU)

Second person is wonderful for inviting your reader to imagine themself in a situation, bringing them close to your topic. A great example is Michelle Cusolito's *Flying Deep*, illustrated by Nicole Wong, which asks children to think about what it would be like if they commanded the submersible Alvin. In this case, second person adds to Cusolito's active voice, making the book feel more interactive.

The active nature of second person may be why it's so popular in how-to text structures. For example, Loree Griffin Burns's *You're Invited to a Moth Ball* uses second person to explain how to put on a moth-viewing party. Again, "you" adds to that active voice.

EXERCISE 18: PRACTICING POV

Could changing your manuscript's point of view add to your voice? As a fun exercise, try rewriting a couple of spreads from your book using a different POV. Then evaluate how the voice and emotion have shifted. Would this work for your entire draft?

TENSE AND VOICE

Verb tense also can affect the voice and mood of your picture book. Most picture books are written in simple past tense or present tense. Each tense creates different effects. Here are some snippets we've seen before from *The Fire of Stars*:

Revision 1

Young Cecilia spent hours outside watching slimy slugs slink through her garden, picking out constellations in the night sky, and counting trees among her best friends.

She planned to be a botanist, a plant scientist. She would research and discover new things all on her own. Her greatest fear was that everything would be figured out by the time she grew up. Lucky for Cecilia, she lived in a time when science changed everything.

Revision 2

Cecilia spends hours
watching slimy slugs glide through the garden
and making friends with trees and flowers ...

Cecilia realizes all by herself why an orchid has a petal like a bee's belly.

To trick the bees, of course!

Did you detect the difference in the verb tense? I switched my story from simple past tense ("Cecilia spent/planned/lived") to present ("Cecilia spends/realizes"). How does that shift the voice and mood of the piece?

I think present tense adds to the sense of immediacy and wonder. It is one more way to put the reader in the scene, where they can watch the action unfold minute by minute.

In my examples, I've stated everything as fact. In grammar, that's called the indicative mood. But that's not the only way we can write in present or past tense.

For an unusual example of present tense, see Patricia MacLachlan's *The Iridescence of Birds: A Book about Henri Matisse*, illustrated by Hadley Hooper, which beings, "If you were a boy named Henri Matisse, who lived in a dreary town in northern France ..." The whole book is hypothetical, and MacLachlan writes it in what's called the subjunctive mood.

Consider how changing verb tense or mood could alter the voice of your picture book. If you are looking for some inspiration, check out Oklahoma State's "Five Grammatical Moods," linked on the resources page of my website. And for a more thorough discussion of verb tense, see the link for Grammarly on the same resources page.

EXERCISE 19: SHIFTING TENSE AND MOOD

Just for fun, rework a couple of spreads or scenes from your picture book in a different tense or mood. What do you think? How does it shift the voice of the manuscript? How does it make you feel? Is it something you might want to try moving forward?

YOUR TURN: THE VOICE-LEVEL REWRITE

It's time for the last of our three major rewrites. Once you finish this rewrite, everything else is small tweaks. I promise.

Take out your work in progress and your responses to the previous exercises.

- Consider: What voice or mood do you want to create for your reader?
- What point of view (POV), tense, and voice would be most appropriate?
- Using the tools you've learned in this section, rework your entire manuscript.
- Make sure to incorporate sound devices, rhythm, and figurative language to paint pictures for your reader, as well as vivid verbs and sensory details.

When you've finished, I hope you have some ice cream on hand, because it's time to celebrate this tremendous accomplishment.

SECTION 5: PERFECTING PACING

CHAPTER 15

TAUT TENSION AND PERFECT PACING

f you write fiction picture books for readers ages 4 to 8, you have probably heard the common advice that your manuscript must be 500 words or fewer. I have heard fellow writers say that nonfiction picture books should be 1,200, 1,000, or even 800 words or fewer.

While most agents and editors probably would not accept a 6,000-word picture book, you have some wiggle room with word count. Agent and nonfiction author Miranda Paul notes in her blog post, "Picture Book Word Count, and Other Rules That Are Meant to Be Broken," that nonfiction picture books for older readers (ages 7 and up) can often run 2,000 words or longer. For Paul, the key consideration is whether the length is appropriate for your age group.

In my experience, the second consideration is whether your story feels long to the reader. A long story can feel shorter if it is well-paced and keeps the reader excitedly turning pages. Pacing is critical, no matter your word count.

After reading Chapter 15, you will:

- Understand the connection between tension and pacing
- Review the story elements that influence pacing
- Learn techniques that drive page turns

THE WORD COUNT CONUNDRUM

Despite the common advice to write shorter nonfiction picture book texts, I've never received feedback from an editor or agent about a book's specific word count. What I have received feedback about is pacing.

When my agent, Lara Perkins, took *Wood, Wire, Wings* out on submission, the main text was approximately 900 words. Carolyn Yoder at Calkins Creek Books was interested, but she didn't think the book was quite ready to be acquired (and it wasn't). Yoder asked me to revise and resubmit.

As I revised, the draft ballooned to 2,000 words. That's the version that sold. Yoder and I made further adjustments, including cutting some redundant text after Tracy Subisak finished her illustrations. The final book weighs in at 1,300 words. The entire time, Yoder was focused not on the word count but on tension and pacing.

A longer manuscript written in scenes with vivid voice and tension can pull an eager reader through the pages. Reading it goes by in a flash. Meanwhile, a short manuscript with little tension, where a writer has summarized and skipped scenes, can drag. Pacing is key.

PACING AND TENSION: SOME DEFINITIONS

Pacing is how quickly the story moves for the reader. Fast-paced books like thrillers entice readers to eagerly turn pages. Readers read slow-paced books (or sections) more leisurely. Literary fiction often falls into the category of books with a slower pace.

Pacing is tightly connected to tension. According to the NY Book Editors website, tension means anticipation. Readers keep reading if you've built anticipation for what will happen next.

Pacing and tension aren't necessarily consistent throughout a book. They rise and fall to create an experience for the reader. Even the most fast-paced thriller occasionally gives the reader a chance to rest and regroup before the next big action scene.

PACING AND TENSION TECHNIQUES YOU ALREADY KNOW

You've already learned several tools in the previous chapters that contribute to the tension and pacing of your book. Let's review them quickly.

Structure (Section 2)

Some story structures have built-in tension. Books that use a narrative structure raise questions like "What's going to happen next?" and "Will the main character achieve their goal?" Likewise, a question-and-answer structure sets up a consistent pattern: first a question is introduced, and then it is answered. That consistency shapes reader expectations and keeps them turning pages. Problem-solution structure also taps into reader anticipation. Once a problem is introduced, readers are encouraged to read on to see how the problem will be solved.

For story structures without built-in tension, like list structure or compare-and-contrast structure, we always have to think about ordering our examples for maximum reader anticipation. This may mean introducing another level of organization to draw the reader through the story, like the changing seasons or the hours in a day, or organizing examples from most conventional to most unexpected.

Writing in Scenes (Chapters 8 and 9)

Writing in scenes also affects pacing and tension. Vivid verbs and sensory details, as well as a character's internalizations, put a reader in the scene and make them feel as if the story is happening to them. Scenes can pick up the pace—even though scenes are frequently longer than straightforward summary. Scenes create tension as the reader watches the minute-by-minute action unfold and wonders what will happen next. Conversely, portions of a book written in summary frequently have a slower pace and less tension.

Voice Tools (Chapters 11 and 12)

The tools that define your book's voice also contribute to its pacing. Remember how punctuation, sound devices like assonance and alliteration, and vowel and consonant sounds create legato or staccato affects. Legato writing creates a slower pace, while staccato quickens the pace. Likewise, repetition (like a refrain) creates reader expectations and anticipation, building tension.

Now that we've reviewed the tools you already know, let's look at a few more tools authors have for creating tension that drives page turns. These are especially helpful in expository books without a main character or a narrative arc.

TEASE A MYSTERY

Every book is a kind of mystery. In narrative books, the mystery is "Will the main character succeed?" In books without main characters, the mystery is often implied. It's more like "Will the author prove their point or takeaway?" And that takeaway is often explained by the title or the first spread.

But authors can also be more direct about setting up a mystery in the opening spreads. Elizabeth Shreeve's *Out of the Blue: How Animals Evolved from Prehistoric Seas*, illustrated by Frann Preston-Gannon, is an excellent example. The first page challenges kids to guess which two animals are most closely related: hippos, dolphins, or sharks. Shreeve then says the answer lies in prehistoric seas. Kids must read the entire book to learn the answer to the question posed on that first page.

GUESSING GAMES

Author and agent Miranda Paul sets up a guessing game in *Whose Hands Are These?* Each spread describes a member of the community and what they do with their hands. But their job is a secret. Kids must turn the page to learn the answer to the repeated question "Whose hands are these?" Miranda also uses rhyme, which shapes kids' guesses. Readers know the answer has to rhyme. I can imagine rooms full of kids shouting their guesses out loud as they turn each page.

PUNCTUATION TO DRIVE PAGE TURNS

Punctuation is another technique to control pacing and build tension. It's one I used frequently in *The Fire of Stars*, often spreading sentences across page turns so the reader must turn the page to finish reading the sentence. This creates moments of anticipation.

Here's an example you've seen before:

Pages 10–11

Soon everything shifts and separates—

Mother trades the soil and starry country skies
　　for the sooty smokestacks of London
　　where Cecilia's brother Humfry can attend a better school.
　　Cecilia is forced to say hello to city streets full of strangers and
　　good-bye to the company of trees and bees.
　　The change is crushing — [turn to pages 12–13]

Throughout the book, ellipses or em dashes lead readers to the next page. One student cleverly likened the three dots of an ellipse to the "dun dun dun" musical phrase used to emphasize dramatic moments in TV shows.

Rhetorical questions are another punctuation technique that can create anticipation and drive page turns. Candace Fleming uses them cleverly in *Honeybee*. On several spreads, she presents a repeated rhetorical question: "Is it time for flying?" The reader must turn the page to find the answer.

DON'T GIVE AWAY THE ENDING

To maximize tension and page turns, you need to be careful about giving away the ending of the scene or the entire book. If readers know how the book or scene ends, they won't feel any anticipation. For example, *Wood, Wire, Wings* begins with a snapshot of Lilian Todd's character:

Example 1

To Emma Lilian Todd, problems were like gusts of wind. They set her mind soaring.

What if I had started the book this way instead?

Example 2

In 1910, Emma Lilian Todd became the first woman to design a working airplane on her own. And here's how she did it.

What do you notice about the two examples? Which one makes you want to keep reading? In Example 2, I've told the reader the end of the book right up front. Why would they want to keep reading? The joy of reading a narrative is to experience the main character's journey and to see if they will succeed and how they'll do it.

You also have to be careful not to give away the ending in your scenes by telling the reader how the scene ends through a topic sentence. For example, compare these two scenes:

Example 3

Another day [Lilian] took apart the clock, spreading the pieces before her. Did this wheel fit here? Did that lever fit there? She put the pieces back this way. No tick. She put the pieces back that way. No tock. The clock stayed still. Failure! Lilian stood baffled but buoyed by the challenge.

What if I had written it as follows?

Example 4

Lilian refused to give up when she couldn't figure things out. One day she took apart the clock, spreading the pieces before her. Did this wheel fit here? Did that lever fit there? She put the pieces back this way. No tick. She put the pieces back that way. No tock. The clock stayed still. Failure! Lilian stood baffled but buoyed by the challenge.

What do you think? With the first sentence in Example 4, I give away the point of the entire scene. Reader anticipation in this scene comes from wanting to know how Lilian responds to a challenge. If I tell you right away instead of letting you read and find out, the tension evaporates.

I find not giving away the ending to be particularly hard at the scene level. Most of us are used to writing nonfiction essays, which always have a topic sentence that summarizes the main idea of the paragraph. Then we provide our evidence. But when writing a picture book, it often works better to provide the evidence and then give the topic sentence at the end to reinforce the point the scene has made.

Let your readers' questions pull them through the scene—and the entire book. Don't give them the answers to their questions up front. That's no fun!

EXERCISE 20: TENSION AND PACING PICTURE BOOK STUDY

Grab a nonfiction picture book off your shelf and look at some of the pacing and tension techniques we've covered. Analyze:

- Does the structure have built-in tension? If not, how are the examples organized for maximum tension and page turns?
- Do scenes add to the tension? How?
- What voice tools does the author use to control pacing and tension? Consider:
- Staccato versus legato effects

- Repetition
- Rhythm and rhyme
- What mystery is set up in the beginning of the book?
- Does each scene pose a new question?
- Does the author use punctuation like ellipses or em dashes to drive page turns? What about rhetorical questions?
- Has the author given away the ending anywhere?
- What is your overall impression of the book?

EXERCISE 21: PACING AND TENSION IN YOUR WORK IN PROGRESS

Look at your work in progress and consider the pacing and tension elements introduced in this chapter. Then consider:

- What's your book's mystery?
- What questions does the reader want answered?
- Can you use punctuation to drive page turns?
- Have you given away the ending and deflated your tension, either in the whole book or in a particular scene?

Make the adjustments you need to maximize tension and perfect your book's pacing.

CHAPTER 16
IMAGINING ILLUSTRATIONS

When we let illustrations help tell our story, we can tighten our text and quicken our pace. Bogging down the reader with backstory or visual descriptions makes for a boring read and is often unnecessary when the illustrations can do that work for you.

After reading Chapter 16, you will:

- Learn the different jobs illustrations can do
- Practice visualizing the illustrations that might accompany your text
- Understand illustration notes, who they are for, and when you need them

A PICTURE IS WORTH A THOUSAND WORDS

"The drawing shows me at a glance what would be spread over ten pages in a book."—Ivan Turgenev, *Fathers and Sons* (1862) (translation by Constance Garnett)

As I mentioned before, *Wood, Wire, Wings* sold at almost 2,000 words but currently clocks in at closer to 1,300.

What changed? A few things, but a significant change was eliminating words that became redundant once Tracy Subisak finished the illustrations.

The before and after are below. Example 1 is what was sent to Tracy to illustrate. Example 2 is what appeared in the finished book once the redundant text was removed.

Example 1

Lilian was born in 1865 during the Industrial Revolution, an age of invention. As she was growing up, newspapers across America brimmed with stories of brand-new creations:

Telephones and typewriters.

Subways and sewing machines.

Inventions to make life faster, safer, or easier.

It seemed like everyone was tinkering … [49 words]

Example 2

Lilian grew up in a time when it seemed like everyone was tinkering. [13 words; the text accompanies a spread showing a number of labeled inventions from that time period]

ILLUSTRATIONS "SHOW, DON'T TELL"

There are many different circumstances where it's more efficient to show through illustrations versus telling with words—that's the power of picture books. I have outlined the most common circumstances for showing instead of telling below.

Setting

A few sensory details within your text can go a long way toward revealing your setting and putting the reader in the scene. You don't have to spend paragraphs describing the setting when the illustrations will show it. Focus your words on senses beyond the visual, like sound, smell, touch, and taste.

Character Physical Descriptions

If you are writing history or biography, you don't have to tell the reader what your main character looks like. Their hair and eye color will be shown in the illustrations. Same goes for books about plants and animals.

Historical Context

Often, when we're writing about big topics like social injustice, child readers need a certain amount of historical context. Yet this background information doesn't all have to be conveyed through words. Illustrations can carry a lot of the burden, as they did in my example from *Wood, Wire, Wings* above.

Look at books like Rob Sanders's *Pride: The Story of Harvey Milk and the Rainbow Flag*, illustrated by Steven Salerno. The text is simple and understated. Sanders writes that some people didn't agree with Harvey Milk. Then, rather than explain why in the text, he leaves it to Steven Salerno to illustrate people in the crowd holding protest signs that reveal their bigotry against gay people. That's enough context for kids. Sanders doesn't need to explain the historic discrimination against LGBTQ+ people and the whole history of their fight for civil rights.

Similarly, in *Bartali's Bicycle: The True Story of Gino Bartali, Italy's Secret Hero* by Megan Hoyt, illustrated by Iacopo Bruno, readers need a bit of context about Hitler and the Nazis to understand Bartali's heroism. Instead of providing this context with words, Hoyt relies on understatement, saying only that the world started to change and "strange ideas" began to spread in Italy. She doesn't mention Hitler or the Nazis by name at all. Instead, illustrator Iacopo Bruno depicts them in the illustrations. That's enough context to understand Bartali's heroism without slowing down the story.

Scientific Concepts

Often illustrations can better explain or help simplify difficult scientific concepts. *Moth: An Evolution Story* by Isabel Thomas, illustrated by Daniel Egnéus, is an excellent example. The book is a case study in natural selection. It's the true story of how the color of peppered moths changed in just a few generations as soot coated English cities during the Industrial Revolution. As the environment changed, the occasional black moth had a higher survival rate and passed its genes on to future generations. Rather than get into a lengthy explanation as I just did, Thomas relies on Egnéus's illustrations to show the advantage of different moth colors as camouflage and how they changed over time.

Likewise, in *The Secret Code Inside You: All about Your DNA*, written by Rajani LaRocca, MD, and illustrated by Steven Salerno, LaRocca provides a very simple explanation of DNA, mostly telling the reader what DNA does. Meanwhile, Steven Salerno's illustrations give more details like where DNA is located and what a cell looks like. None of this information is in the text.

With both historical context and scientific concepts, you must ask:

- "What does my reader *have* to know to make sense of things?"
- "What is age (and understanding) appropriate?"
- And finally, "What's the best way to explain—with words, with pictures, or with a bit of both?"

There's a great quote from Roy Peter Clark in *Tell It Like It Is*: "The best way to deal with difficult information is to leave it out of the story." I couldn't agree more. Keep only the explanations that are critical, rely on illustrations, and leave the rest for the back matter. Otherwise, you'll grind your story to a halt.

Difficult Situations

Illustrations also can be used to deal with difficult situations in kid-appropriate ways. In *Beware the Crocodile* by Martin Jenkins, illustrated by Satoshi Kitamura, Jenkins describes an open-mouthed crocodile heading for its prey. Instead of telling the reader what happens next, illustrator Satoshi Kitamura draws a satisfied crocodile on the next spread with a bulging stomach. The crocodile captured its prey offstage during the page turn. Yet by using the pictures, kids can get the inference. More sensitive kids are spared the gory details, and any blood is left off the page.

A WORD ABOUT ILLUSTRATION NOTES

When necessary, illustration notes explain your overall concept, or what you envision on particular spreads when your text is spare. But despite their name, illustration notes are for your agent or editor, *not* the illustrator. Their sole purpose is to get your idea across when it is not clear from the text alone. Once your book is acquired, the editor and art director will decide whether to share your illustration notes with the illustrator.

Author Tara Lazar calls illustration notes "action notes." I encourage you to read her excellent post on the topic, in which she provides an example from her fiction manuscript. (You'll find the post linked on my resources page.) Here is a nonfiction example of illustration notes, going back to Example 2 above from *Wood, Wire, Wings*:

Example 2

Lilian grew up in a time when it seemed like everyone was tinkering.

If I were submitting this to my agent today using sparser text, I would probably include an illustration note as follows:

Lilian grew up in a time when it seemed like everyone was tinkering.

[Illo. note: Labeled inventions from the Golden Age of Invention, for example the first telephone, first subway, dishwasher, telegraph.]

Note how I've left the direction a bit open ended. An illustrator would be able to exercise their creativity, picking and choosing inventions from the period. I don't need to go into detail about what the inventions look like because either the illustrator will do their own research or the editor will ask me to provide research sources.

Use illustration notes sparingly. Too many illustration notes disrupt the flow of your story and make it difficult to read. You can also opt for including a global illustration note in your query or at the beginning of your manuscript to explain your concept. That is what I did in *The Fire of Stars*. The global illustration note reads as follows:

[*Illo. note: Each spread splits horizontally with the story of the star above and Cecilia's story below.*]

In addition to that global illustration note, I had to provide illustration notes on every page describing the phase of the star's life cycle because the poetic text wasn't quite clear enough for an agent or editor to understand what was happening. For example, "In a cloud of dust and dirt" doesn't tell the illustrator that the page's illustration should depict a nebula.

As you perfect your manuscript, consider what details could be better conveyed by illustrations. Where could you rely on sparser text? Where would understatement have greater impact? What words must you really include for readers to understand the story? There's no better way to test this than by making a book mock-up, called a **dummy**.

EXERCISE 22: MAKING A DUMMY

Print out a copy of your work in progress using only one side of each page (don't print double-sided). If you can, shrink the font to 9 or 10 points and print in two columns, though this step isn't necessary.

You'll also need:

- Scissors
- Tape
- Pencil
- Eight 8.5" × 11" sheets of blank paper (for a thirty-two-page book). If your book is longer than thirty-two pages, add one more sheet of paper for every four pages.
- Stapler

To make the dummy:

- Stack the sheets of 8.5" × 11" paper and turn them so they are oriented horizontally (landscape orientation).
- Fold the stack of paper in half, with the crease running vertically.
- Staple the papers in the crease to create your dummy.
- Number the pages of the dummy in the upper-right corner. Your first page (a single page) is page 3. Then label pages 4–5, 6–7, etc.
- Cut up your printed manuscript into the text blocks you've imagined for each page or spread.
- Use tape to attach the text blocks to the dummy pages.
- Bonus: Draw simple sketches of illustrations you envision or make notes about what can be illustrated on each spread. Don't worry about artistic ability—this is just for you!

After you've made your dummy, evaluate:

- How is your pacing?
- Is your setup happening over too many pages?
- Does your resolution come too soon?
- Are there places where you should take an extra beat to reinforce your tension or takeaway?
- What keeps the reader turning pages?
- How can you rearrange text or add punctuation to better drive page turns?

- Does each spread have something interesting to illustrate? Is there a variety of illustrations?
- Can you eliminate words anywhere and rely on illustrations instead, without losing the flavor of your manuscript?

Move text around as needed until you are happy with the finished product. Then go back to your draft and adjust.

CHAPTER 17
BACK MATTER AND TEXT FEATURES MATTER

Targeted back matter and text features can make a book even more useful in schools, libraries, and at home. In other words, great back matter may just help sell your book.

After you read Chapter 17, you will understand:

- What marketing angles are
- How to use back matter and text features to amp up your marketing angles
- The menu of back matter and text feature options
- How to format back matter and text features in your submission

WHAT'S YOUR (MARKETING) ANGLE?

Imagine the children's section of your local bookstore. It's crowded with books stacked high on tables and organized on shelves. A child eagerly leafs through books on a low shelf, while their parent reads jacket flap copy. What makes a parent or reader pick your book? The answer(s) to that question is your marketing angle. The more angles your book has, the better it will sell.

Let's identify some marketing angles your book might have.

Subject

Sometimes a book's subject gives it built-in kid appeal. For example, *Wood, Wire, Wings* features airplanes. *A True Wonder* is about a superhero. Both are perennial kid-favorite topics, as are trucks, dinosaurs, glitter, and pirates. On her website, author Tara Lazar shares a list of 199 things kids love, which might be helpful the next time you are considering a book subject. You'll find her list linked on the resources page of my website.

Hands-On Component

Many books include hands-on elements, like recipes and activities kids can do after reading the book. This is a great way to extend a book's usefulness at home and to help librarians with story time ideas.

Holidays or Anniversaries

Remember Marcie Colleen's *Survivor Tree*? That's a September 11 book published to coincide with the twentieth anniversary of the tragedy. It was one of three books that came out within months of each other. Recently there has been an uptick in Juneteenth books published around the creation of the new federal holiday. In my house, we have a holiday tradition of reading one winter or Christmas picture book each day during the month of December. It's like a bookish Advent calendar. I buy a lot of Christmas books, and I'm not alone.

Teachers and librarians are always looking for books to use during Women's History Month, Black History Month, Pride Month, and so on.

Curricular Tie-Ins (STEM/Social Studies)

Part of the appeal of *Wood, Wire, Wings* is that it can be used to teach the Next Generation Science Standards (NGSS) engineering design process, which students start learning in kindergarten. Teachers can use *The Fire of Stars* to discuss the traits that make a scientist, like perseverance and curiosity. A book like Miranda Paul's *Whose Hands Are These?* ties into kindergarten community helper units.

Look at curriculum standards in the kindergarten to third-grade range. This is where most of your readers will be. The following resources (all linked on my website) can help you see how your book might fit into content curriculum:

- Next Generation Science Standards
- Common Core State Standards (math)
- Most social studies curricula are state based, so look at your state's or those of larger states like California and Texas.

Concepts

For preschool students ages 3 and 4, consider if your book touches on any concepts typically taught in the curriculum. Preschoolers commonly learn colors, numbers, the alphabet, opposites, and shapes. Could you play up any of these angles in your story or back matter?

Social Emotional Learning Topics

Social Emotional Learning (SEL) topics have become an important part of the school curriculum. These topics include self-management, self-awareness, social awareness, relationship skills, and responsible decision making. *Wood, Wire, Wings* focuses on perseverance and embracing failure, elements that tie into the SEL curriculum under "self-management." Resilience, the takeaway of Marcie Colleen's *Survivor Tree*, also falls under self-management. These SEL topics provide an additional way teachers can use the books in the classroom, increasing the books' marketability. You can learn more about SEL frameworks through these two sources, which are linked on my resources page:

- California Transformative SEL Competencies
- CASEL framework

Voice

Writing lyrically and using poetic techniques, if appropriate for your subject, can add to a book's marketing potential. Teachers and librarians use books written in rhyme for National Poetry Month each April. Any book using figurative language like alliteration, metaphors, and so on can be used to teach Common Core English Language Arts (ELA) standards on those topics. You'll find the Common Core English Language Arts (ELA) curriculum standards linked on my website.

Structure or POV

If you pick an unusual story structure, this alone can set your book apart. The parallel structure and triple-read-aloud potential in *The Fire of Stars* were major selling points. Some structures, like narrative or cause and effect, also tie into curriculum, increasing their usefulness. And sometimes an unusual POV, like smoke in *I Am Smoke*, can be a selling point, too.

EXERCISE 23: ALL THE RIGHT ANGLES

For your work in progress, consider how your book could be used to enhance learning in schools, libraries, and at home. Go through the list above. Brainstorm as many marketing angles as you can.

WORKING THE ANGLES: TEXT FEATURES AND BACK MATTER

How do we enhance marketing angles? Some of them are baked into our subject, structure, or voice, but we can play up others through text features and back matter.

Text features are technically any words not included in the main body of your manuscript, like sidebars, text boxes, and quotations. But the term also includes back matter, the elements that normally come after the main text. For the purposes of our discussion, we will define text features as elements that appear in the main part of the book alongside the story, and back matter as the text that appears at the end of the book after the main story.

TEXT FEATURES

Grab a nonfiction picture book or two off your shelf and flip through the pages. Do you notice any elements that aren't a part of the main text but appear alongside it? *Wood, Wire, Wings* includes quotations pulled from historic newspapers. *A True Wonder* contains mini-biographies of key figures in Wonder Woman's history, formatted like trading cards. What do the books on your shelf include? You may see popular text features like these:

Sidebars

These short bits of text allow older readers to learn more about specific topics covered in the main text. Sometimes sidebars are as short as a sentence or two, as in *The Leaf Detective: How Margaret Lowman Uncovered Secrets in the Rainforest* by Heather Lang, illustrated by Jana Christy. Other times they run longer. Often the text that appears in sidebars could easily be shifted to the back matter. That's what I did in *The Fire of Stars*. Instead of including specific information about each stage of star formation on the main spreads, I placed it all after the main text.

The decision to use sidebars versus back matter is one of tradeoffs. Sidebars can distract from a book's read-aloud factor and flow, but you also must consider when a reader wants certain pieces of information. Will they read the back matter, or will you miss your opportunity to convey the information altogether?

Quotations

As in *Wood, Wire, Wings*, sometimes quotations appear that aren't part of the narrative flow of a story but are related to what's happening on the page. They almost function like sidebars.

In previous chapters I shared the scene where Lilian Todd takes apart the clock as a young girl but can't put it back together. On that same spread, I include the following quote: "Ever since I can remember, I couldn't have a piece of tin or wire in my hands without bending it and twisting it to make something. ..."

That quote gives readers wonderful insight into Lilian Todd's character, but it's not necessary in the context of the scene. If an editor wanted, they could delete the quote entirely and the scene with Lilian Todd taking apart the clock would still make sense.

Timelines

Timelines can run across the tops or bottoms of pages, putting books that cover a lot of ground in historical context. Elizabeth Shreeve's *Out of the Blue* includes this element.

Maps, Charts, or Other Graphics

Aside from the illustrations, sometimes spreads incorporate maps, charts, or graphics. Jason Chin's *Grand Canyon* contains a graphical inset on each spread showing the canyon's rock layers and how they correspond to the geologic time scale. In Melissa Stewart's *Fourteen*

Monkeys, each spread contains a graphic that shows which part of the rainforest canopy the monkey inhabits. Annette Bay Pimentel's *Girl Running: Bobbi Gibb and the Boston Marathon*, illustrated by Micha Archer, includes a map of the Boston Marathon course that runs along the bottom of each spread.

Text Boxes

Text boxes are closely linked to charts and other graphics, but they are text based instead of image based. *Pink Is for Blobfish: Discovering the World's Perfectly Pink Animals* by Jess Keating, illustrated by David DeGrand, includes a text box on each spread with key features of the pink animal discussed.

Primary Sources

Some books contain snippets of primary-source documents, often within the illustrations and apart from the main text. *Write to Me* by Cynthia Grady, illustrated by Amiko Hirao, features both black-and-white historic photographs and letters sent by Japanese American children from the internment camps to their librarian. The latter are recreated in the book's illustrations.

HOW DO WE SUGGEST TEXT FEATURES IN OUR SUBMISSIONS?

No matter the text feature, I format them in the same way in the manuscript. I set them off in brackets, label them appropriately ("sidebar," "quotation," or "text box," for example), and format them in italics. Then I put them right where they would appear in the flow of the story. It's the same way I write illustration notes. Here are some examples:

[*Sidebar: Emma Lilian Todd was born in 1865 in Washington, D.C.*]

[*Quotation: "There is nothing so exasperating as building airplanes."*]

[*Text box:*
    Name: William Moulton Marston

Job: Wonder Woman Creator]

When determining your word count for submission, don't include the word count of text features or illustration notes—only count the words in your main story. If you want, you could include two word counts: one for the main story and one for the text features. For example, you might put this at the top of your manuscript:

Word count: 1,000 words

Sidebars: 500 words

BACK MATTER MATTERS

Much of the same information included as text features could appear instead as back matter. However, don't think of back matter as a mere dumping ground for "the rest of the story" or a place to insert what you had to cut from the main story. Strong back matter adds to the marketability of your book by highlighting the many ways your book can be used in the classroom and at home. Think carefully about how to enhance the reading experience, extend the learning, and highlight your marketing angles, especially curriculum tie-ins. School and library markets are critical for successful nonfiction.

Grab a nonfiction picture book or two off your shelf and flip to the back matter. What elements do you see? *Wood, Wire, Wings* includes an author's note, a timeline of aviation milestones, and a selected bibliography. *The Fire of Stars* includes an author's note, a timeline of Cecilia Payne's life, and a deep dive into the star formation process. What do the books on your shelf include?

Here are some of the more common back matter options:

Author or illustrator notes. These are a great place to share how you got your story idea, as well as your research and/or illustration process and why this story matters to you, all of which tie into ELA curriculum.

Timelines. These put your story into historical or scientific context.

Additional information. This could include additional facts about the animals, plants, or concepts from the main text, especially if you don't want the information cluttering up your story. It's the same information that might appear in a sidebar. In *The Fire of Stars*, I included additional information on the star formation process.

Activities and recipes. These provide hands-on opportunities to extend the learning introduced in the main book. For example, in *Fry Bread*, Kevin Noble Maillard offers his recipe for "Kevin's Fry Bread," which kids can make.

Things kids can do. These are especially popular in activism or conservation books to show kids how their actions can contribute to making a big difference in the world.

Photographs. I love to include historic photos of the people I write about. Keep careful notes about where you found the photographs and who owns them. Once you have a publishing contract, you'll need to get permission from the copyright owner to include the photographs in your book. This may involve paying a licensing fee. For more information see *Law and Authors* by Jacqueline D. Lipton.

Suggested reading. Sometimes authors include lists of books or websites for young readers to learn more about the subject. These should be children's books and kid-appropriate websites versus resources geared for adult readers.

Selected bibliographies. These show the mix of primary and secondary sources you used in your research. Not only do bibliographies add to the credibility of your work, but they also model an author's research process for young writers in the classroom learning to do the same.

Glossaries. These define domain-specific words in the text. In books that include foreign languages, the glossary provides translations.

Back matter is typically counted in the pages it takes up instead of words. A 350-word author's note will take up about one page. Make sure to account for back matter when dummying your book. If you've taken a full thirty-two pages to tell the main story, you haven't left yourself room to amp up your marketing angles. Save room for your back matter.

SUBMITTING BACK MATTER

Technically speaking, back matter doesn't have to be finished before submission. You could submit a list of back matter ideas. However, many agents and editors want to see your back matter as part of your submission.

Agent Jennifer Laughran of the Andrea Brown Literary Agency says if the back matter adds context to the story, then she wants to see it because she feels that's "part of the story." If the back matter is simply supplementary, like a map where a specific plant grows, then she feels it's less important. I've linked to her full post on this topic on the resources page of my website.

I take a "better safe than sorry" approach and always submit back matter. When submitting it, I include the header "Optional Back Matter" in my manuscript and then include all the back matter. I typically don't include a page or word count for this material.

EXERCISE 24: AMPING UP THE ANGLES

Go back to the list of potential marketing angles you generated in "Exercise 23: All the Right Angles." What are the top two or three angles you think would add to your book's marketability and usefulness? Now look through the list of text features and back matter options in this chapter. What elements would best enhance your angles? You can't include everything, so make a few careful choices. And remember: back matter is likely to change once your book is acquired.

SECTION 6: GETTING READY TO SUBMIT

CHAPTER 18
FINDING FEEDBACK

Learning to self-edit and revise is an important skill. Still, it can be difficult to see shortcomings or holes in your work, no matter how diligently you've analyzed and revised it. Once you've revised your nonfiction picture book with the help of this book, it's time to solicit feedback from other writers. There is nothing like getting a set of fresh eyes on your work.

After reading Chapter 18, you will:

- Understand the different types of critique groups and how they operate
- Learn how to connect with fellow writers for critiques
- Know how to get the most out of a critique
- Know when your work is ready to submit

CONNECTING THROUGH CRITIQUES

I formed my first critique group in 2012. That year I joined Julie Hedlund's 12x12 Picture Book Challenge. Several of us decided to form an ongoing group to give each other feedback on our manuscripts as we learned the craft of writing picture books. We called ourselves the Awesome Picture Book Group (APBGers for short). Over the years, a few members have joined and left, but the group remains. It's still my first stop to get feedback on my work, or to check in and ask questions as they arise.

I'm also part of a second critique group focused on nonfiction. It's important to have some critique partners experienced in writing both nonfiction and picture books, since each has its own conventions.

TYPES OF CRITIQUE GROUPS

Critique groups operate in many different ways. Here are a few common formats:

Real Time (in Person or Online)

Many critique groups meet in person or over a video conference platform, often on a monthly schedule. Work is typically due a week or two before the established meeting date so everyone has time to read and consider the manuscripts before the session. During the meeting, each manuscript is given a set amount of time for discussion, maybe twenty or thirty minutes. During that time, fellow authors share their feedback orally on the draft. Depending on the group, people might also send along written comments.

The benefit of getting oral feedback in real time is that it quickly becomes clear which aspects of a manuscript aren't working. When problems are diagnosed, an in-person critique group provides a live opportunity to ask follow-up questions and brainstorm solutions.

However, this type of critique group comes with a potential downside: if no one in the group swaps written comments, authors must take furious notes to capture all the feedback. You might consider recording the session if it's held over a video conference.

Written Critiques

Some groups swap written comments and don't have regular meetings. These swaps might be done on a schedule or whenever manuscripts are ready.

These groups can work well for folks with busy schedules. They are also a good fit for writers who better formulate their thoughts on a manuscript through writing rather than verbal feedback. With written feedback, an author receiving the critique can easily refer to the comments when revising.

The potential downside with a written critique group is that it may be tough to get critiques back in a timely manner unless you set formal deadlines. For example, groups may decide everyone submits work by the first of the month and shares written comments via email on the fifteenth of each month. It's important to set deadlines for comments when you send out your manuscript for critique. One other potential downside is if you are only sharing written comments, then there's no opportunity to brainstorm solutions.

When submitting manuscripts, you could trade emails, use a shared Google Drive account, or even upload files to a private Facebook group that acts as a virtual watercooler where people can hang out and chat. You could also use a platform like Slack to upload manuscripts and engage in discussion.

WHERE TO FIND CRITIQUE GROUPS

Here are a few ideas for where to find and connect with critique partners. You'll find links to these resources on my website:

- **Classes and webinars.** These are a great way to connect with like-minded authors intent on improving their craft. If the class is in person, you can circulate a sign-up sheet for interested writers to provide an email address. If the course is held online, you could put a note in the chat asking those interested in a critique group to contact you through your email address. This is how I formed a couple of my critique groups, connecting through classes I took at The Writing Barn and other places.
- **Facebook groups.** Check out some of these Facebook groups to connect with critique partners. KidLit411 has a dedicated critique swap group that's separate from the main group. Sub It Club also has a critique partner matchup group on Facebook.

- **The Society of Children's Book Writers and Illustrators (SCBWI).** If you are an SCBWI member, you can connect with other writers through local meetups called Schmoozes. These aren't critique groups per se, but they are a way to meet writers in your area who may want to form a group. SCBWI also maintains a section of its message board where you can post work for critique.
- **Your agent (if you have one).** As an agented author, you could reach out to your agent to see if their agency has other clients seeking a group.
- **A debut or promotional group.** If you have published a book and are part of a promotional group, you might find like-minded people in your marketing group who want to form a critique group.
- **Paid groups.** There are several paid options for critique groups. Author Marcie Colleen offers "Study Hall," a monthly critique group where authors can submit and polish one manuscript a week for feedback from Marcie and the others in the group. The platform Inked Voices is another option. Paid critique groups aren't permanent and ongoing, though you may be able to form friendships with authors in the group and continue critiquing each other's work when the session is over.

ADVICE ON FINDING AND GETTING CRITIQUES

Many authors have shared a lot of wonderful advice on giving and getting critiques. Ann Whitford Paul's *Writing Picture Books* includes a helpful chapter. What I want to share is some less-common advice:

- **Your work can benefit from feedback at all stages.** Your work doesn't have to be perfectly polished to get a critique. We can all benefit from feedback—even on story ideas and concepts. And if something is nagging you in a draft, share it!

- **Ask questions to help your critique partners focus their feedback.** You often know what your draft needs or where the potential problems lie. It really helps your critique partners if you submit a few questions at the top of your draft. Your notes might say something like, "Is this point of view working?" "How is my world building?" or "Is the end dragging?" By focusing the feedback, you are ensuring what you get is useful. Otherwise, people often feel compelled to critique something, and what you get back may not be as helpful. Diana Ma and Christina Scheuer call this process "collaborative feedback." I've linked to an article about their process on my resources page.

- **Have your partners read for the elements we've covered in this book.** They could consider your takeaway, structure, scenes, voice, pacing, and so on. These are the elements I brainstorm with clients during coaching sessions, and they tend to be the most common areas where we all need help.

- **Check for commonalities in the critiques.** After you get feedback, let it sit for a bit. Then consider if there are commonalities among the comments you received. Focus on the problems highlighted versus the solutions offered. The solutions may be less helpful. Yet if everyone focused on a specific element—for example, that they didn't get a sense of time and place from your text, or they were unclear about your takeaway—it's probably worth digging into. Remember, it's possible to get a bad critique where your partner just doesn't get what you are trying to do. It happens. But when many people are pointing out the same issues with your book, you need to pay attention.

- **Giving critiques helps you grow, too.** There is no better way to grow as a writer than to diagnose what's working and what's not in manuscripts. Giving thoughtful critiques will help you grow your craft.

ARE YOU READY TO SUBMIT?

Have you polished your picture book manuscript until it shines? Are you ready to send your story to an agent or editor? Before you hit "send" on your first query, I encourage you to step back for a moment and make sure you are truly ready to query.

Before you query agents, you typically need three polished picture books. Yup, you heard that right. Authors writing middle grade or young adult (YA) can query with one book, but in picture book land, it's not enough to have one knockout picture book. You need to have three equally amazing stories that an agent feels they could sell almost immediately (although they will likely ask you to revise all of them). One exception is if you are an author/illustrator. They typically can submit a single story, which includes a finished dummy and illustration samples. If you already write longer works, like middle grade or YA, you also don't need to have three polished picture books. One middle grade and one picture book is fine, too.

"But wait," you say. "You only query one picture book at a time." You are completely right. You send each agent the one book you think is the best match for their taste. However, at the end of your query, make sure to mention you have "additional picture books available upon request." If the agent likes the initial manuscript, they will ask you to send at least two more.

If those two additional manuscripts are not as polished as the first, you are setting yourself up for rejection. And if you really love that agent and want to query again after waiting a few months, you can't send any of the three manuscripts they've already seen. You will need to start over.

So how do you know if your three manuscripts are ready to submit? Ask these questions before you start querying agents:

1. Have you made your story the best it can be? This includes making sure you've studied the market to see what's being published right now. Have you read your book aloud? Have you dummied your book to make sure it contains the right

amount of text on each spread and has enough illustration possibilities?

2. Have your stories been critiqued by fellow authors, either in a critique group or through a critique forum or manuscript swap? See earlier in this chapter for how to form critique groups.

3. Have you done substantial revision after each round of critiques? "Substantial" means using the critiques to completely reimagine your story. This may mean changing the POV or voice, reworking scenes, and rethinking the overall structure. Revising is not about breaking out the thesaurus and swapping a few words. It's about rewriting, as you've learned throughout this book.

4. Have you sought professional feedback? Once your drafts have made it through your critique group and subsequent revisions, it's time to seek out the next level of feedback. Here are some sources for finding that feedback.:

- Consider signing up for an agent or editor critique at a conference. Agents and editors know the market intimately, and aside from providing feedback on your writing, they can also give you a sense of how your book might be received in the market.
- Pay a professional picture book author for a critique. You'll find my services linked on my website.
- Sometimes critiques are offered as part of a webinar or picture book writing class.
- You also can submit to contests, which are judged by agents, editors, and authors. A contest win is a strong indication your work is ready to submit, or very close.
- Finally, don't overlook services like Rate Your Story to determine if your stories are submission ready. And if they aren't, take heart. Simply take the feedback and go back to Step 1.

Repeat Steps 1 through 4 as many times as necessary.

Getting books from first draft to submission ready can take years. It took me four years of writing, taking classes, reading craft books, and getting critiques before I had three submission-ready picture books. You might work faster or slower. But the bottom line is to make sure you are submitting your best work possible to give yourself the best chance of success.

If you are ready to sell your stories through an agent or directly to editors, it's time for the next chapter.

CHAPTER 19
SELLING YOUR STORY

You've received feedback from your critique group and revised with the help of this book. You've also received a positive critique from an agent or editor suggesting your story is ready to go. What's the next step? Selling your story.

After reading Chapter 19, you will:

- Know the benefits of submitting to agents versus editors
- Have a list of editors who are open to unagented submissions
- Know how to research agents
- Know how to write a query letter for nonfiction picture books

AGENTS VERSUS EDITORS

Before we discuss the pros and cons of sending your work to a literary agent or directly to an editor at a publishing house, let's look at what both of these people do. An editor acquires your book for the publisher and acts as the book's project manager, coordinating the edits, art, production schedule, and marketing. On the other hand, a literary agent acts as a middleperson between the author and the publisher or editor. Agents receive a commission, normally 15 percent of the author's royalties, for their services. Many publishers, particularly larger publishers, will only accept manuscripts sent to them through an agent. Once a manuscript is accepted, the agent negotiates the contract with the publishing house, eliminating the need for a literary lawyer.

So, should you query an agent or submit your work directly to an editor? This is a very personal choice, but I've included some pros and cons to consider. If you are planning to make a career of writing for children, you might consider an agent. Here's why:

- Many publishers these days will not accept unagented submissions.
- Even for publishers who do accept unagented submissions, your agent likely will be able to negotiate a higher advance payment, which will more than cover their commission.
- An agent will help you negotiate your contracts, looking not just at money but also at clauses that could hamper your ability to build a career, like restrictive options, noncompetes, and so on.
- Agents review royalty statements for accuracy and intercede on your behalf on all sorts of things: you hate your cover design, your editor is asking for changes you don't agree with, or you haven't seen a marketing plan for your book.
- Many agents also will help you prioritize your projects, and some even provide editorial feedback.

Querying editors directly might be for you if:

- You only envision publishing one or two books.
- Your book is on a very specific topic and not necessarily attractive to major publishing houses. In these instances, you might go directly to publishers. You will have fewer publishers open to you, but author Bitsy Kemper keeps a sizable list, which you'll find linked on my website.

- You've queried agents with the book, and they've all rejected it. At that point, you might as well submit it to editors on your own.

At the time of this writing, the market for picture books is extremely tough. Many more authors are opting to skip querying agents and send their work directly to smaller publishers. If you decide to go that route, you need a literary lawyer to review your contracts. Join The Authors Guild for free access to literary lawyers who can review your contract and provide feedback. If you would like a lawyer to represent you in negotiations, you can hire a literary lawyer directly.

CREATING A QUERY

Whether you choose to pursue agents or editors, you must draft a query letter. My favorite advice on how to write a query comes from a Sub It Club post on the basic query letter breakdown, which is linked on my website. Essentially, your query letter has three components, "the hook" (your pitch), "the book" (details about the book like age range, category, and word count), and "the cook" (your bio). For nonfiction books, it's also important to include a sentence or two in the "book" section that speaks to your depth of research.

- Were you able to interview your main character's descendent or a prominent scientist working on your topic?
- Did you dig into your character's journals or read scientific journals?
- Has your work been reviewed by a subject matter expert who gave it their approval?
- Do you have access to original images that could be used in the back matter?

A sentence or two about the depth of your research can help sell your book. You can find a couple of nonfiction "query letters that worked" on the Sub It Club site, including my query for *Wood, Wire,*

Wings and my analysis of Hannah Holt's *The Diamond and the Boy* query.

FINDING AGENTS

Once you have three perfectly polished picture book manuscripts and a query letter, you are ready to build a list of agents to query. These tips will help get you started; you can find links to related resources on my website.

Start with a Strong List

Before you begin your in-depth research, seek out a foundational list of agents accepting picture books from a reliable online source:

- Author Heather Ayris Burnell maintains the Monster List of Picture Book Agents.
- You can also start with a list at QueryTracker.net. Membership is free, though paying twenty-five dollars per year will give you access to more data on agents. As a free member, I searched under the picture book category and got a list of 237 agents accepting picture books.
- The Association of American Literary Agents website contains a "find an agent" section where you can search by category and genre.
- The Children's Book Academy maintains a list of more than a hundred picture book agents.
- Another source is Publishers Marketplace, a paid service that costs twenty-five dollars per month. However, one month is probably enough time to access all the data you need on agents you want to query. In Publishers Marketplace, go to the "Dealmakers" portion of the database. Select "Browse Top Dealmaker Lists" and select the word "agents" and the category "picture book nonfiction." This will generate a list of the top one hundred agents—those reporting the most deals—in the picture book nonfiction category.

- Subscribe to *Publishers Weekly*'s "Children's Bookshelf," a free, twice-weekly newsletter that includes book deal announcements. In the announcements, you'll find the names of the literary agents who brokered the deals.

Keep Your Eye Out for New Agents

New agents come on the scene all the time and can present a wonderful opportunity since they often are looking to build their roster of clients. Pay attention to new agents joining well-established agencies. Until an agent establishes their own reputation with editors, they are trading on the reputation of their agency.

You might also consider new agents transitioning from editorial positions at well-respected publishing houses. They will have contacts at publishers and a good idea of what sorts of books are selling in the current market. No matter an agent's background, make sure they are being mentored by a senior agent as they learn the ropes. To find new agents, subscribe for free to *Publishers Weekly*'s "PW Daily" newsletter. Each edition includes a "Job Moves" section, and you'll find new agents listed there.

Research the Agents

While resources like Publishers Marketplace require subscriptions to access, don't forget about the host of free information available to you, too. QueryTracker.net aggregates many of the information sources below:

- Often the agency website will include a bio about the agent, as well as information about what type of work the agent is looking for.
- The 12x12 Challenge website has wonderful interviews with agents who have agreed to take part in the 12x12 Picture Book Challenge.
- Manuscript Wish List has a list of agents with lots of information, too. On X (formerly Twitter) you can also follow the #mswl and #pb hashtags to find agents tweeting about picture books they'd like to see.

- Literary Rambles posts agent spotlights. You can follow the blog and search past posts.
- If you have the name of an agent, plug it into the search function on *Publishers Weekly* to pull up past deals, so you can learn about clients and types of publishers the agent sells to. When looking at an agent's deals, see if they are selling work to publishers you envision for your own books. Are they selling to reputable publishers like the Big Five, plus smaller publishers like Chronicle, Scholastic, Astra, and so on? Or are they mostly selling to publishers you could access on your own?
- Google the agent's name plus the word "interview." Often agents grant blog interviews, which will give you an idea of what they are looking for.
- You also can follow agents on X to get a sense of their taste, but for heaven's sake, don't tweet to them about the status of your query.
- If you are an SCBWI member, check out their annual publication *The Book: The Essential Guide to Publishing for Children*, which includes a whole section on children's book agents. The information is basic but worth skimming.

Keep Track of Your Queries

You can keep track of agents and your queries in a simple Excel spreadsheet, or you can use a service like QueryTracker, which allows you to track your queries online. If you are building your own spreadsheet, make note of the agent's name, the agency, when you queried, which manuscript you queried, how you queried (snail mail, email, form), average response time, and response. I also put links in my spreadsheet to online sources of information about the agent. You can find my sample spreadsheet on the resources page of my website.

Beware of Predators

Double-check agents on sites like Writer Beware and the forums on Absolute Write. Not all agents are on the up-and-up. If an agent asks for money up front, like fees to read or evaluate your manuscript, or if they steer you toward paid editorial services, these are red flags.

Andrea Brown Literary Agency agent Jennifer Laughran warns against "schmagents" (agents who are just plain bad at their jobs) and shares some red flags in a post you'll find linked on my site.

Getting an agent (or a book deal) is a numbers game, and it can take dozens or even a hundred queries before you find the right agent for your work. Only query people you want to work with, but make sure to cast your net widely. Don't get hung up on one or two dream agents. Your true dream agent is one who is passionate about your work and has the ability to sell it.

SOME PARTING ADVICE

The world needs your stories. Your book, the one you are revising right this very minute, is going to change some kid's life. That child will read your book by flashlight under the covers or carry it like a security blanket in their backpack.

All you have to do is keep going. Revising isn't magic; it's a set of learned skills. And now you have all the tools you need to figure out what your book should be, what you need to change, and how to do it. It just takes patience and time.

It's been my honor to be a small part of your journey. Please keep in touch and let me know how it goes! You can find me at KirstenWLarson.com (where you can follow my blog or sign up for my newsletter) and on social media @kirstenwlarson.

Remember, all articles and resources mentioned in this book can be found on my website at www.KirstenWLarson.com/NFPBLinks.html. If you find any errors or broken links in this book or have suggestions for what you'd like to see included in future editions, please let me know.

And if you've found this book helpful, please recommend it to a friend or share your review on the book platform of your choice. I'd really appreciate it.

Happy writing and revising!

AFTERWORD

It's been my honor to be a small part of your journey. Please keep in touch and let me know how it goes! You can find me at www.Kirsten-WLarson.com (where you can follow my blog or sign up for my newsletter) and on social media @kirstenwlarson.

Remember, all articles and resources mentioned in this book can be found on my website at https://KirstenWLarson.com/NFPBLinks/. If you find any errors or broken links in this book or have suggestions for what you'd like to see included in future editions, please let me know.

And if you've found this book helpful, please recommend it to a friend or share your review on the book platform of your choice. I'd really appreciate it.

Happy writing and revising!

APPENDIX A: GLOSSARY

Acquire: When a publisher buys rights to a manuscript with the intention of publishing it

Back matter: Information that appears in the back of your book, after the story is finished. In picture books, these often include the author's or illustrator's notes, timelines, bibliographies, glossaries, suggested reading, and other elements.

Character arc: A change in the main character from the beginning to the end of a story

Chronological: Arranged in time order, typically from oldest to newest

Critique groups: A group of serious writers who exchange writing work regularly for the purposes of giving and receiving feedback

Dummy: A book mock-up that contains text and rough sketches

Ellipses: Three periods (…) signifying an incomplete thought

Em dash: A double hyphen (—) used to signify a break in a sentence

Expository literature: Books on narrowly defined topics that "feature an innovative format and carefully chosen text structure, a strong voice, and rich, engaging language" (Melissa Stewart)

Filter words: Extraneous words that call attention to the filtering of thoughts or actions through a character. These words typically have to do with the five senses, like "felt," "heard," "saw," or "smelled."

Flat arc: A story in which the main character doesn't change but changes the people or world around them

Figurative language: Words or phrases that are meaningful but not literally true. Metaphors and similes are examples of figurative language.

Informational fiction: A book whose primary purpose is to inform the reader about a topic from science, history, etc. but uses made-up elements, like a fictional narrator or an invented storyline

Internalization: A character's internal thoughts and emotional reactions

Jacket flap copy: The marketing copy on the inside left flap of the book jacket

Legato: In music, in a long, flowing manner without breaks

Lyrical voice: Writing that is poetic and evocative, with a song-like quality

Narrative: A series of connected events with a beginning, middle, and end; a story

Pacing: How fast or slow the story (or part of the story) is moving

Pitch: A short, memorable sentence or two used to describe your book

Query letter: A one-page cover letter that includes your pitch, details about your book, and your biography. A query letter is sent to agents along with your manuscript when you are trying to get a literary agent.

Revise and resubmit (R&R): When an agent or editor likes your manuscript but believes it needs more work, they may ask you to revise it and send it back to them. This is known as an R&R.

School and library nonfiction: Books produced for use in school and classroom libraries versus sold in bookstores. These books often are published in series and written at specific reading levels so children can read the books on their own. They often have special bindings that hold up to heavy use.

Spread: Two facing pages of a book

Staccato: In music, when each note is played sharply and is distinct from the others

Stakes: What is at stake for a character in a book; what will be gained or lost

STEM: An acronym for "science, technology, engineering, and math"

Story beat (or beat): A single moment or point of action in a book that shifts the direction or tone

Story spine: Originally developed by Kenn Adams, this story structure is used extensively by Pixar

Story structure: In a book, the order in which you present the scenes or examples

Submission: Sent to book editors to see if they will acquire the book

Tension: A reader's anticipation, concern, or curiosity about what will happen next in a book. This is a key element that keeps readers turning pages.

Text features: Supplementary information that appears alongside the main text and adds to the reader's understanding, like diagrams, maps, definitions, sidebars, or text boxes

Trade market: Books primarily sold to booksellers and wholesalers versus directly to the public. These publishers include the "Big Five" publishers like Penguin Random House and Simon and Schuster, as well as midsize and smaller publishers like Chronicle Books and Astra.

APPENDIX B: FEATURED NONFICTION PICTURE BOOKS

Animal Architects by Amy Cherrix, illustrated by Chris Sasaki

Bartali's Bicycle: The True Story of Gino Bartali, Italy's Secret Hero by Megan Hoyt, illustrated by Iacopo Bruno

Because of an Acorn by Lola M. Schaefer and Adam Schaefer, illustrated by Frann Preston-Gannon

Before She Was Harriet by Lesa Cline-Ransome, illustrated by James E. Ransome

Beware the Crocodile by Martin Jenkins, illustrated by Satoshi Kitamura

Bird & Diz by Gary Golio, illustrated by Ed Young

Birds of a Feather: Bowerbirds and Me by Susan Roth

Bobcat Prowling by Maria Gianferrari, illustrated by Bagram Ibatoulline

Bone by Bone: Comparing Animal Skeletons by Sara Levine, illustrated by T. S. Spookytooth

The Diamond and the Boy: The Creation of Diamonds & the Life of H. Tracy Hall by Hannah Holt, illustrated by Jay Fleck

The Fire of Stars: The Life and Brilliance of the Woman Who Discovered What Stars Are Made Of by Kirsten W. Larson, illustrated by Katherine Roy

Flying Deep: Climb Inside Deep-Sea Submersible Alvin by Michelle Cusolito, illustrated by Nicole Wong

Fourteen Monkeys: A Rainforest Rhyme by Melissa Stewart, illustrated by Steve Jenkins

Freaky, Funky Fish: Odd Facts about Fascinating Fish by Debra Kempf Shumaker, illustrated by Claire Powell

Fry Bread: A Native American Family Story by Kevin Noble Maillard, illustrated by Juana Martinez-Neal

Girl Running: Bobbi Gibb and the Boston Marathon by Annette Bay Pimentel, illustrated by Micha Archer

Give Bees a Chance by Bethany Barton

Glitter Everywhere!: Where It Came From, Where It's Found & Where It's Going by Chris Barton, illustrated by Chaaya Prabhat

Grand Canyon by Jason Chin

A History of Underwear with Professor Chicken by Hannah Holt, illustrated by Korwin Briggs

Honeybee: The Busy Life of Apis Mellifera by Candace Fleming, illustrated by Eric Rohmann

How to Build an Insect by Roberta Gibson, illustrated by Anne Lambelet

I Am Smoke by Henry Herz, illustrated by Mercè López

If Bees Disappeared by Lily Williams

If You Give a Mouse a Cookie by Laura Numeroff, illustrated by Felicia Bond

If You Take Away the Otter by Susannah Buhrman-Deever, illustrated by Matthew Trueman

The Important Thing about Margaret Wise Brown by Mac Barnett, illustrated by Sarah Jacoby

The Iridescence of Birds: A Book about Henri Matisse by Patricia MacLachlan, illustrated by Hadley Hooper

Jazz Day: The Making of a Famous Photograph by Roxane Orgill, illustrated by Francis Vallejo

Jumbo: The Making of the Boeing 747 by Chris Gall

The Leaf Detective: How Margaret Lowman Uncovered Secrets in the Rainforest by Heather Lang, illustrated by Jana Christy

Lincoln and Kennedy: A Pair to Compare by Gene Baretta

Martin & Mahalia: His Words, Her Song by Andrea Davis Pinkney, illustrated by Brian Pinkney

Meow!: The Truth about Cats by Annette Whipple

Mesmerized: How Ben Franklin Solved a Mystery That Baffled All of France by Mara Rockliff, illustrated by Iacopo Bruno

The Mess That We Made by Michelle Lord, illustrated by Julia Blattman

Mimic Makers: Biomimicry Inventors Inspired by Nature by Kristen Nordstrom, illustrated by Paul Boston

Moth: An Evolution Story by Isabel Thomas, illustrated by Daniel Egnéus

Muslim Girls Rise: Inspirational Champions of Our Time by Saira Mir, illustrated by Aaliya Jaleel

The Nest That Wren Built by Randi Sonenshine, illustrated by Anne Hunter

The Next President by Kate Messner, illustrated by Adam Rex

No Monkeys, No Chocolate by Melissa Stewart and Allen Young, illustrated by Nicole Wong

No Voice Too Small: Fourteen Young Americans Making History edited by Lindsay H. Metcalf, Keila V. Dawson, and Jeanette Bradley; illustrated by Jeanette Bradley

'Ohana Means Family by Ilima Loomis, illustrated by Kenard Pak

Out of the Blue: How Animals Evolved from Prehistoric Seas by Elizabeth Shreeve, illustrated by Frann Preston-Gannon

Over and Under the Waves by Kate Messner, illustrated by Christopher Neal

Pink Is for Blobfish: Discovering the World's Perfectly Pink Animals by Jess Keating, illustrated by David DeGrand

Pipsqueaks, Slowpokes, and Stinkers: Celebrating Animal Underdogs by Melissa Stewart, illustrated by Stephanie Laberis

Plants Can't Sit Still by Rebecca E. Hirsch, illustrated by Mia Posada

Pride: The Story of Harvey Milk and the Rainbow Flag by Rob Sanders, illustrated by Steven Salerno

The Secret Code Inside You: All about Your DNA by Rajani LaRocca, MD, illustrated by Steven Salerno

Survivor Tree by Marcie Colleen, illustrated by Aaron Becker

Tiny Creatures: The World of Microbes by Nicola Davies, illustrated by Emily Sutton

A True Wonder: The Comic Book Hero Who Changed Everything by Kirsten W. Larson, illustrated Katy Wu

Water Is Water by Miranda Paul, illustrated by Jason Chin

We Are Still Here!: Native American Truths Everyone Should Know by Traci Sorell, illustrated by Frané Lessac

Whose Hands Are These?: A Community Helper Guessing Book by Miranda Paul, illustrated by Luciana Navarro Powell

Wood, Wire, Wings: Emma Lilian Todd Invents an Airplane by Kirsten W. Larson, illustrated by Tracy Subisak

Write to Me: Letters from Japanese American Children to the Librarian They Left Behind by Cynthia Grady, illustrated by Amiko Hirao

You're Invited to a Moth Ball: A Nighttime Insect Celebration by Loree Griffin Burns, illustrated by Ellen Harasimowicz

APPENDIX C: MENTOR TEXT STUDY GUIDE

Throughout this book, I've encouraged you to read mentor texts to study various writing craft elements. Studying mentor texts can teach us so much about structure, voice, beginnings, endings, and so on.

It's best to pick books published in the last five years for mentor texts. This worksheet is a compilation of the elements to notice when studying a mentor text. You can find an electronic, downloadable version on my website: www.KirstenWLarson.com/NFPBLinks.html.

Mentor text title:
  Author:
  Illustrator:
  Publisher:

TAKEAWAY (CHAPTERS 2, 3)

- What is the book's takeaway (Chapter 2)?
- How does the takeaway influence the scenes or examples included in the book (Chapter 3)?

STRUCTURE (CHAPTERS 4–7)

- What story structure does this book employ (Chapters 4–6)?
- Use Debbie Ridpath Ohi's template or draw your own rectangles and thumbnail the text following the directions in Chapter 4, Exercise 4.
- If the book uses a narrative structure, note:
- Who is the main character?
- What is the main character's life like before the inciting incident? How many spreads does the author use to set that up?
- What is the inciting incident—the moment everything changes and the main character embarks on their quest? Where does it fall in the book?
- What does the main character want more than anything else in the world?
- Describe a couple of struggles (and failures).
- Is there an "all is lost" moment where the main character almost throws in the towel? If not, what's the lowest moment? On what spread does it occur?
- How is the main character's life changed at the end? How does this change link to the takeaway?
- Compare and contrast the opening and closing spreads or scenes. What do you notice?
- Do kids appear in this book? If not, how does this text connect with the child reader? What's its kid appeal?
- What are some learnings you can apply to your work in progress?
- If your book uses a different nonnarrative structure (chronological or nonchronological), consider:
- What is the takeaway?
- What are some things you noticed by thumbnailing this book?
- What work does the first spread do?
- What work does the last spread do?
- How are examples ordered?

- Does the book use a secondary structure like night-to-day, following the seasons, or something else?
- Do kids appear in this book? If not, how does this text connect with the child reader? What's its kid appeal?
- What are some learnings you can apply to your work in progress?

SCENES (CHAPTER 8)

- Does this book use scenes? If so, look for evidence of:
- Physical action (especially unfolding in real time)
- Internalization (internal thoughts and emotions, either explicitly stated or suggested)
- Speech
- Sensory details that speak to all five senses—what we can see, hear, touch, taste, and smell
- Vivid verbs
- What effect do the scenes have?
- What emotional response do the scenes evoke for you?

VOICE (CHAPTERS 11–14)

- How would you characterize the voice of this book?
- What elements contribute to the voice of the book? Consider:
- Sound devices like alliteration, assonance, etc. (Chapter 11)
- Punctuation (Chapter 12)
- Figurative language (Chapter 13)
- Sensory details and vivid verbs (Chapter 13)
- What is the book's point of view and verb tense, and how do they contribute to the voice or mood of the book? (Chapter 14)

TENSION AND PACING (CHAPTER 15)

- Does the book's structure have built-in tension? If not, how are the examples organized for maximum tension and page turns?
- How do scenes add to the tension?
- What voice tools does the author use to control pacing and tension? Consider:
- Staccato versus legato effects
- Repetition
- Rhythm and rhyme
- What mystery is set up in the beginning of the book?
- Does each scene pose a new question?
- Does the author use punctuation like ellipses or em dashes to drive page turns? What about rhetorical questions?
- Has the reader given away the ending or maintained the mystery?

ILLUSTRATIONS (CHAPTER 16)

- What work do the illustrations do compared to the text?
- Are there moments where the author has been able to pull back on their words and let the illustrations do the showing?

BACK MATTER AND TEXT FEATURES (CHAPTER 17)

- Does this book have any special marketing angles or tie-ins (to holidays, curriculum, etc.)?
- What back matter and text features does this book have?
- How do they add to the marketing angles or usefulness of the book?

APPENDIX D: THE STEP-BY-STEP REVISION PROCESS

Once you've reconnected with your story and made the decision to revise, you are ready to work through my step-by-step revision process. You will find an electronic version available for download on my website: www.KirstenWLarson.com/NFPBLinks.html.

YOUR TAKEAWAY (CHAPTER 2)

- What do you want readers to remember when they close your book? Go beyond just the facts here.
- What do you want them to feel or do in response to your story?
- In the words of Lisa Cron in *Story Genius*, "What's your point?"
- Is this takeaway important to a child? In other words, does it have kid appeal?
- Now write your takeaway to summarize the point you are making and why kids should care.
- Does information from your research support your takeaway?

- Do kids appear in this book? If not, how does this book connect with the child reader?

STRUCTURE BRAINSTORM (CHAPTERS 3–6)

- Does your topic or takeaway naturally lend itself to a specific structure? If so, which one? (See the list in Appendix E.)
- Brainstorm two or three structures that might work for your story and jot them down in your notebook. If you think your current structure is working well, you can keep it as one of your structures with a goal of improving it.
- Sit with your potential structures for a bit. Does one of them excite you or fill you with possibilities more than the others? That might be your first choice for trying one out.
- Does the prospect of writing a story using any of these structures fill you with dread?
- Listen to your gut and your instincts as you pick a structure to try out.
- Is there a natural secondary layer of organization that might help your story, like seasons, day-to-night, or the engineering design process?

STRUCTURE REWRITE (CHAPTER 7)

- Thumbnail two to three mentor texts that use your desired structure.
- Thumbnail your book, thinking about how your book's ideas will unfold spread by spread.
- Write a new draft from scratch using only your thumbnails as a guide and without looking at your research.
- Keep your text as short as possible. Imagine yourself reading it out loud to a child.
- Focus on feelings, not facts.

- Remember, if you get stuck, try writing your pitch first and then expand it into thumbnails.

SCENES (CHAPTERS 8–10)

- What parts of your story should be written as scenes for maximum tension and emotion? Look back at Chapter 8, where I discussed some key moments you might consider writing in scene.
- What parts of your story can you summarize?
- For the portions you've identified that need to be in scene, rewrite the book one scene at a time.
- For each scene, first let the scene play out in your mind like a mini-movie, imagining the voiceover narration.
- Write the text for that voiceover. That's your scene.
- Now evaluate. Use colored pens, highlighters, or boxes/squiggles/underlines to indicate physical actions, internalization, speech, sensory details, and vivid verbs.
- See if you can insert "because of that" between each cause and effect. Does every action or choice have a cause, which produces an effect and leads to the next action?
- Are your causes and effects in the proper order so you don't confuse your reader?
- If causes and effects don't make sense, do you need to add internalization? Remember the proper order: physical reaction internalization speech (or physical action).
- Does each scene begin with an implied question? Is that questioned answered through the scene, logically leading to a new question?
- Is your scene a mini-arc that produces a small change in your main character or the reader? Does it add to the overall arc of the story?
- Highlight and then remove any filter words and creative dialogue tags.
- Take the time to locate the research sources you need for authentic motivation, dialogue, and sensory details.

Footnote where you found those details so you don't have to do it later.

VOICE (CHAPTERS 11–14)

- What voice or mood do you want to create for your reader?
- What point of view (POV), tense, and voice would be most appropriate?
- Using the tools I've shared, rework your entire manuscript using:
- **Sound devices:** Working spread by spread, use Thesaurus.com and Rhymezone.com to incorporate sound devices like alliteration and assonance.
- **Rhythm:** Consider how the punctuation and words you've chosen add to the voice and mood of your book.
- **Figurative language:** Add metaphors and similes as appropriate, along with vivid verbs and sensory details to paint mental pictures.
- **POV:** Consider first-, second-, and third-person points of view.
- If necessary, to get into voice, type out a passage from a book that uses the same voice you are striving for, or use one of our warmups like writing a brevette or making a Word Ladder.

PACING (CHAPTERS 15, 16)

- What mystery is set up in the beginning of the book?
- Does your structure have built-in tension? If not, how are the examples organized for maximum tension and page turns?
- How is your pacing? Does each scene or spread add to the tension and pose a question for the reader, encouraging them to turn the page?

- Is there anywhere you've given away the ending and deflated your tension, either in the whole book or in a particular scene?
- Following the instructions in Chapter 16, create a book dummy, taping your text onto the pages. Then consider:
- Is your setup happening over too many pages?
- Does your resolution come too soon?
- Is there somewhere you should take an extra beat to reinforce your tension or takeaway?
- How can you rearrange text or add punctuation to better drive page turns?
- Does each spread have something interesting to illustrate? Is there a variety of illustrations?
- Can you eliminate words anywhere and rely on illustrations instead without losing the flavor of your manuscript?
- Make adjustments for maximum tension and perfect pacing.

BACK MATTER AND TEXT FEATURES (CHAPTER 17)

- Brainstorm some marketing angles for your book, like holidays or curricular tie-ins.
- What back matter and text features would enhance your marketing angles and your book's usefulness?
- Consider the list of back matter and text feature options in Appendix F.

APPENDIX E: NONFICTION STRUCTURE OPTIONS

You will find an electronic version available for download on my website: www.KirstenWLarson.com/NFPBLinks.html.

CHRONOLOGICAL (ORDERED BY TIME)

Narrative Structure

- A main character
- A story goal, quest, or problem, kicked off by an inciting incident
- Struggles and failures
- A lowest moment
- A change in the main character from beginning to end, known as the **character arc**

Parallel Narrative Structure

- Two main characters (humans, inanimate objects, or one of each)
- A story goal, quest, or problem

- Struggles and failures
- A lowest moment
- A change in the main characters from beginning to end, known as the **character arc**

Cumulative Structure

- Often follows the rhythmic pattern of the children's rhyme "The House That Jack Built"
- Accumulates information; as new blocks are added, all those that came before are repeated. For example, "This is the house that Jack built" (Block 1), followed by "This is the malt" (Block 2) "that lay in the house that Jack built" (repeat Block 1). Visually it looks like this:

1

21

321

4321

- Good for books that show how choices, changes, or events accumulate

Cause-and-Effect Structure

- Often has one or more spreads setting up the idea of cause and effect and hinting at the takeaway
- Each supporting example causes the next
- Think of this structure as a chain of dominoes all lined up. Visually it looks like this:

12

23

34

45

- Often uses words like "because," "as a result," "resulted," "caused," "affected," "since," "due to," "effect," and "if" / "then"
- Used to show how one small change or event can set off a chain reaction that ripples and grows

Circular Structure

- Begins and ends in the same place, with a slight variation
- Frequently uses repetition to track the cycle
- Especially appropriate for books about natural cycles (e.g., life cycles, the water cycle, or the rock cycle)

Reverse Structure

- Moves one way in time, but backward chronologically, from the oldest event or information to the newest
- Often uses key words like "before" or "before that" to remind readers they are stepping back in time
- Good for stories where you want to peel back the layers of an onion to get to a central idea. You can also think of this structure like opening a set of Russian nesting dolls.

Problem-Solution Structure

- Sets up a problem and then offers the solution
- Often used as a secondary structure layered over a narrative (as in *Mesmerized*) or a list structure (as in *Mimic Makers*)
- May use key words like "propose," "solution," "answer," "issue," "problem," "problematic," "remedy," "prevention," and "fix"
- A flexible structure suitable for STEM topics and histories or biographies

How-to Structure

- Used for step-by-step processes (like recipes)
- Gets the reader actively involved in the book
- May use words that give cues about the order of things, like "first," "next," "before," "lastly," and "then"

NONCHRONOLOGICAL (NOT TIME ORDERED)

Description ("All About" Books)

- Gives a broad overview of a topic versus just a slice
- Examples need some form of order, whether levels of importance, what the reader needs to know first, second, etc., or something else
- Encyclopedias also use description structure, so exercise extra caution to avoid making your book too encyclopedic.
- Must have something else that makes the book truly stunning, perhaps the voice, takeaway, or illustration potential

List Structure

- The first spread often explains the concept, with each subsequent spread providing an example.
- The final spread often reinforces the takeaway.
- Examples must be ordered for maximum tension and page turn.
- Can be used for STEM books but also collective biographies and moments in time from multiple perspectives

Compare-and-Contrast Structure

- As with a list book, the first spread often explains the concept and subsequent spreads provide examples.
- Can compare and contrast people, inanimate objects, or both
- May compare just two subjects (like *Lincoln and Kennedy*) or fourteen or more (like types of fish or uses of feathers)

- Must explain how the subjects are alike and different; some comparisons may take place in the illustrations
- May use key words like "like," "unlike," "both," "neither," "similar," and "different"
- The final spread often reinforces the takeaway.

Question-and-Answer Structure

- The first spread often explains the concept, while subsequent spreads provide examples.
- Simulates a reader's natural curiosity, offering an interactive element
- Questions may be asked on one spread and answered on another, driving page turns.
- The final spread often reinforces the takeaway.

OTHER OPTIONS

- The sky's the limit! Ideas include:
- Overlapping (e.g., *The Next President*)
- Epistolary (e.g., *Write to Me)*
- A structure suggested naturally by your subject, like engineering design or the scientific method

APPENDIX F: BACK MATTER AND TEXT FEATURE OPTIONS

You will find an electronic version available for download on my website: www.KirstenWLarson.com/NFPBLinks.html.

TEXT FEATURES

- Sidebars
- Quotations
- Definitions
- Text boxes
- Timeline
- Maps, charts, other graphical features
- Excerpts from primary sources within illustrations

BACK MATTER OPTIONS

- Author's note
- Illustrator's note
- Timeline
- Additional information about topics covered in the book

- Activities, recipes, or things kids can do
- Primary-source photographs
- Glossary
- Suggested reading
- Selected bibliography

ABOUT THE AUTHOR

Kirsten W. Larson used to work with rocket scientists at NASA. Now she writes award-winning books for curious kids. Kirsten lives near Los Angeles with her husband, two sons, and dog, Chloe. Learn more and sign up for her newsletter at www.KirstenWLarson.com.